Paul Silvia blends psychological rese[...]
anecdotal evidence, and practical "h[...]
terrific primer that lives up to its title. Silvia not only
writes a lot, but he also writes very well (indeed, this is
the rare academic book that will have you laughing out loud).
If writing is your Achilles' heel as a researcher or if you simply
want to be more prolific, this is the book for you!
—James C. Kaufman, PhD, Director, Learning Research
    Institute; Department of Psychology, California State
    University at San Bernardino

Paul Silvia's new book is just the tonic for academics who
want to be more productive. Silvia demolishes all of the
typical excuses that people use to put off getting to work,
and he gives a few concise, practical tips that will help
anyone to write more. Psychologists are the target readers,
but professors in any discipline would benefit from the
advice in this book.
—R. Keith Sawyer, PhD, Associate Professor, Department of
    Education, Washington University, St. Louis, MO

A contemporary admonition tells us, "If you talk the talk,
you have to be able to walk the walk." Paul Silvia does
both; he writes effectively about how to write effectively.
Without being either a scold or a Pollyanna, he identifies
ways in which each of us can achieve our goals of being
more proficient authors.
—Lawrence S. Wrightsman, PhD, Professor of Psychology,
    University of Kansas, Lawrence; author of The Psychology
    of the Supreme Court and coauthor of Forensic
    Psychology (2nd ed., with Sol Fulero)

A common complaint among faculty and graduate students alike is that writing often takes a backseat to other professional and personal commitments. For those who have trouble writing enough, Paul Silvia explains how to write more. For those who already write plenty, he shows how to do so more efficiently and with lower cost to one's other obligations. Every researcher will benefit from the gems of advice in this book.

—*Mark R. Leary, PhD, Professor of Psychology and Neuroscience, Duke University, Durham, NC*

How to Write a Lot should be titled *How to Write a Lot and Write It Well.* Full of practical wisdom and entertaining examples, the book is both informative and fun. I'd recommend it to all students and colleagues who must either publish often or sadly perish.

—*Dean Keith Simonton, PhD, Distinguished Professor of Psychology, University of California, Davis; recipient of the William James Book Award of the American Psychological Association*

How to Write a Lot

How to Write a Lot

A Practical Guide to Productive Academic Writing

Paul J. Silvia, PhD

American Psychological Association • *Washington, DC*

Second Printing, April 2007
Third Printing, November 2007
Fourth Printing, August 2008

Published by
APA Life Tools
American Psychological Association
750 First Street, NE
Washington, DC 20002
www.apa.org

To order	Tel: (800) 374-2721; Direct: (202) 336-5510
APA Order Department	Fax: (202) 336-5502; TDD/TTY: (202) 336-6123
P.O. Box 92984	Online: www.apa.org/books/
Washington, DC 20090-2984	E-mail: order@apa.org

In the U.K., Europe, Africa, and the Middle East, copies may be ordered from
American Psychological Association
3 Henrietta Street
Covent Garden, London
WC2E 8LU England

Typeset in Minion and Goudy by World Composition Services, Inc., Sterling, VA

Printer: Sheridan Books, Ann Arbor, MI
Cover Designer: Naylor Design, Washington, DC
Technical/Production Editor: Harriet Kaplan

The opinions and statements published are the responsibility of the authors, and such opinions and statements do not necessarily represent the policies of the American Psychological Association.

Library of Congress Cataloging-in-Publication Data

Silvia, Paul J., 1976–
    How to write a lot : a practical guide to productive academic writing / by Paul J. Silvia.— 1st ed.
        p. cm.
    Includes bibliographical references and index.
    ISBN-13: 978-1-59147-743-3
    ISBN-10: 1-59147-743-3
    1. English language—Rhetoric.   2. Academic writing.   I. Title.
    PE1408.S48787 2007
    808'.042—dc22   2006023493

British Library Cataloguing-in-Publication Data
A CIP record is available from the British Library.

Printed in the United States of America
First Edition

This book is dedicated to Beate; thanks for the many morning lattés and for everything else.

Contents

Preface

How to Write a Lot isn't a scholarly book—it's a light-hearted, personal, practical book for a scholarly audience. College professors write in quiet desperation: Writing is hard, and the standards for publication and grant writing are higher than they used to be. Graduate students write in loud, vocal desperation: They struggle with their theses and dissertations while being advised by professors who often struggle with writing, too. A lot of people grapple with fitting writing into a frenetic semester, managing their time, and staying motivated in the face of criticism and rejection. Many people never learned the nuts and bolts of submitting papers to journals, revising manuscripts for resubmission, or working with coauthors.

Writing productively is a skill, not a genetic gift, so you can learn how to do it. This book will show you how to make writing routine and mundane. It presents strategies for writing during the normal work-week, writing with less stress and guilt, and writing more efficiently. If you have a deep backlog of data, if you worry about finding time to write, or if you would like writing to be easier, this book will help.

I'm lucky to have colleagues who like to talk about writing and who tolerate interruptions. Many people took part in my informal surveys of authors and editors, commented on early drafts of this book, and provided encouragement for what must have sounded like a weird project. Big thanks go out to Wesley Allan, Janet Boseovski, Peter Delaney, John Dunlosky, Mike Kane, Tom Kwapil, Scott Lawrence, Mark Leary, Cheryl Logan, Stuart Marcovitch, Lili Sahakyan, Mike Serra, Rick Shull, my dad Raymond Silvia, Jackie White, Beate Winterstein, Ed Wisniewski, and Larry Wrightsman. Lansing Hays and Linda McCarter at APA Books deserve thanks for helping a wobbly first draft grow into a much better book.

The only thing that a writer's room needs, according to Stephen King (2000), is "a door which you are willing to shut" (p. 155). This book is for Beate, my best friend on the other side of the door.

How to Write a Lot

1

Introduction

How to Write a Lot is about becoming a reflective, disciplined writer—it isn't about cranking out fluff, publishing second-rate material for the sake of amassing publications, or turning a crisp journal article into an exegetical exposition. Most psychologists would like to write more than they do, and they would like writing to involve less stress, guilt, and uncertainty. This book is for them. I take a practical, behavior-oriented approach to writing. We won't talk about insecurities, feelings of avoidance and defensiveness, or inner mental blocks that hold people back. We won't talk about developing new skills, either—you already have the basic skills needed to write productively, although you'll improve with practice. And we won't talk about unleashing your inner anything: Put your "inner writer" back on its leash and muzzle it.

Instead, we'll talk about your outer writer. Writing productively is about actions that you aren't doing but could easily do: making a schedule, setting clear goals, keeping track of your work, rewarding yourself, and building good habits. Productive writers don't have special gifts or special traits—they just spend more time writing and use this time more efficiently (Keyes, 2003). Changing your behavior won't necessarily make writing fun, but it will make writing easier and less oppressive.

WRITING IS HARD

If you do research, you probably enjoy it. Research is oddly fun. Talking about ideas and finding ways to test your ideas is intellectually gratifying. Data collection is enjoyable, too, especially when other people do it for you. Even data analysis is fun—it's exciting to see if a study worked. But writing about research isn't fun: Writing is frustrating, complicated, and un-fun. "If you find that writing is hard," wrote William Zinsser (2001), "it's because it *is* hard" (p. 12). To write a journal article, you need to cram complex scientific ideas, methodological details, and statistical analyses into a tight manuscript. It isn't easy, especially when you know that anonymous reviewers will thrash that manuscript like a dusty carpet.

Because collecting data is easier than writing about data, many professors have dark backlogs of studies. They intend to publish those data "someday"—"some decade" is more realistic. Because they struggle with writing, professors yearn for 3-day weekends, spring breaks, vacations, and the summer months. But on the Tuesday after a 3-day weekend, people groan and grumble about how little they wrote. In a big department, the 1st week after summer break is a din of lamentation and self-reproach. This sad cycle of yearning and disappointment begins anew as people search for the next big block of time. Psychologists usually find these big blocks on the weekends, evenings, and vacations. Writing usurps time that should be spent on important leisure activities like spending time with friends and family, making lentil soup, or knitting the dog a Santa hat.

And, as luck would have it, the standards for writing are higher than ever. More psychologists are sending more papers to more journals; more researchers are competing for a shrinking pool of grant money. Deans and department chairs expect more publications than before. Whereas the cheery Provosts of Christmases Past were happy if faculty happened to submit a grant, the grim Provosts of Christmases Present expect new faculty to submit grants. Some departments now require faculty to *receive* a grant as a condition of promotion and tenure. At research-oriented colleges and universities, poor productivity is why people fail to receive tenure or promotion. Even small teaching-oriented colleges have raised their expectations for scholarly publications. It's a hard time to start a career in academic psychology.

THE WAY WE LEARN NOW

Writing is a skill, not an innate gift or a special talent. Like any advanced skill, writing must be developed through systematic instruction and practice. People must learn rules and strategies and then practice them (Ericsson, Krampe, & Tesch-Römer, 1993). Psychology has discovered that deliberate practice breeds skill, but it hasn't applied this knowledge to the training of writing. Compare the teaching of writing with the teaching of other professional skills. Teaching is hard, so we train our graduate students how to do it. Students commonly take a "teaching psychology" seminar and practice teaching by serving as teaching assistants. Many graduate students serve as teaching assistants every semester and become skilled teachers. Statistics and research methods are hard, so we have students take several semesters of advanced classes on these topics, taught by experts in methods and statistics. After many semesters, some students become sophisticated methodologists.

How does psychology train graduate students to write? The most common model of training is to presume that graduate students will learn about writing from their advisors. But many students' advisors are struggling writers who themselves complain about not finding time to write, who pine for spring break and the summer months—the bland are leading the blind. It isn't their fault: Like the students they advise, most college professors had to learn writing "on the street." Some departments teach writing as part of professional skills classes. Although valuable, these classes ignore the motivational struggles of writing and focus instead on grant-writing and the basics of style.

After the students leave graduate school, they won't have an advisor to hound them about their half-finished manuscripts—they'll need the skills to start and finish projects on their own. It's sad, I think, that we expect more from the next generation of writers but fail to train to meet our higher standards.

THIS BOOK'S APPROACH

Academic writing can become a sordid drama. Professors feel oppressed by half-done manuscripts, complain about cruel rejections from journals, scramble breathlessly to submit grant proposals the day before the deadlines, fantasize about the halcyon summer days of writing, and curse the foul start of the semester for stunting their productivity. Psychology is dramatic enough already—we don't need this kind of drama. All of these practices are bad. Academic writing should be more routine, boring, and mundane than it is. To foster a mundane view of writing, this book says nothing about the "soul of writing," the nondenominational "spirit of writing," or even the secular "essence of writing." Only poets talk about the soul of writing. You should write like a normal person, not like a poet and certainly not like a psychologist. And this book says nothing about anyone's insecure feelings of "defensiveness" and "avoidance"; go to your local bookstore's self-help section for that. *How to Write a Lot* views writing as a set of concrete behaviors, such as (a) sitting on a chair, bench, stool, ottoman, toilet, or patch of grass and (b) slapping your flippers against the keyboard to generate paragraphs. You can foster these behaviors using simple strategies. Let everyone else procrastinate, daydream, and complain—spend your time sitting down and moving your mittens.

While you read this book, remember that writing isn't a race or a game. Write as much or as little as you want. Don't feel that you ought to write more than you want to write, and don't publish fluffy nonsense just for the sake of publishing. Don't mistake psychologists who have a lot of publications for psychologists with a lot of good ideas. Psychologists publish articles for many reasons, but scientific communication is the best reason. Publication is the natural, necessary endpoint of the scientific process. Scientists communicate through the written word, and published articles form psychology's body of knowledge about what people are like and why they do what they do. I suspect that most psychologists feel thwarted as writers—they would like to write more, and they'd like writing to be easier— and this book is for them.

LOOKING AHEAD

This short book provides a practical, personal look at how to write a lot. In chapter 2, we scrutinize some of the bad reasons people give for not writing. We'll attack these specious barriers by showing that they have no effect on how much you write. The chapter introduces the strategy of allotting time to write by making a writing schedule. Chapter 3 provides motivational tools for sticking to your writing schedule. You'll learn how to set good goals, to use priorities to manage many projects at once, and to monitor your writing progress. To bolster your new habits, you can start a writing group with some friends. Chapter 4 shows you how to start an *agraphia group*—a social support group for fostering constructive writing habits—for fun and profit. Chapter 5 describes strategies for writing well. Well-written papers and grant proposals stand out from the greasy masses of mediocre papers and proposals, so you should strive to write as well as you can.

Chapters 6 and 7 apply the principles of writing a lot. Chapter 6 gives a practical, in-the-trenches view of writing articles for psychology journals. We may not like reading scientific articles, but we must write them. Prolific writers told me how they write articles, and editors of major journals told me what they want to see in an article. Chapter 6 discusses common questions about mundane aspects of publishing, such as how to write cover letters to editors and how to work with coauthors. Chapter 7 describes how to write scholarly books, because psychology has few resources for aspiring book writers. I provide a personal look at how to write books and describe how to work with publishers. Chapter 8 concludes this brief book with some encouraging words.

2

Specious Barriers to Writing a Lot

Writing is a grim business, much like repairing a sewer or running a mortuary. Although I've never dressed a corpse, I'm sure that it's easier to embalm the dead than to write an article about it. Writing is hard, which is why so many of us do so little of it. If you're reading this book, you probably know how it feels to be thwarted. When I talk with professors and graduate students about writing, they always mention certain barriers. They want to write more, but they believe that there are things holding them back. I call these *specious barriers*: At first they appear to be legitimate reasons for not writing, but they crumble under critical scrutiny. This chapter looks at the most common barriers to writing a lot and describes simple ways to overcome them.

SPECIOUS BARRIER 1

"I can't find time to write," also known as "I would write more if I could just find big blocks of time."

This specious barrier is destined for academia's hall of fame. We've all used this one; some thwarted writers have elevated it to a guiding life theme. But this belief is specious, just like the belief that people use only 10% of their brains. Like most false beliefs, this barrier persists because it's comforting. It's reassuring to believe that circumstances are against you and that you would write a lot if only your schedule had a few more big chunks of time to devote to writing. And your friends around the department understand because they have a hard time finding time to write, too. It's oddly soothing to collude with your colleagues, to bask collectively in the cold glow of frustration.

Why is this barrier specious? The key lies in the word *find*. When people endorse this specious barrier, I imagine them roaming through their schedules like naturalists in search of Time To Write, that most elusive and secretive of creatures. Do you need to "find time to teach"? Of course not—you have a teaching schedule, and you never miss it. If you think that writing time is lurking somewhere, hidden deep within your weekly schedule, you will never write a lot. If you think that you won't be able to write until a big block of time arrives, such as spring break or the summer months, then you'll never write a lot. *Finding time* is a destructive way of thinking about writing. Never say this again.

Instead of *finding* time to write, *allot* time to write. Prolific writers make a schedule and stick to it. It's that simple. Right now, take a few moments to think about the writing schedule that you want to have. Think about your week: Are there some hours that are generally free *every week*? If you teach on Tuesdays and Thursdays, maybe Monday and Wednesday mornings are good times to write. If you feel energized in the afternoon or evening, maybe later times would work well for you. Each person will have a different set of good times for writing, given his or her other commitments. *The secret is the regularity, not the number of days or the number of hours.* It doesn't matter if you pick 1 day a week or all 5 weekdays—just find a set of regular times, write them in your weekly planner, and write during those times. To begin, allot a mere 4 hours per week. After you see the astronomical increase in your writing output, you can always add more hours.

When we talk about writing schedules, most people ask me about my schedule. (Some people ask defiantly, as if expecting me to shrug and say "Well, sticking to a schedule is easier said than done.") I write Monday through Friday, between 8:00 a.m. and 10:00 a.m. I wake up, make coffee, and sit down at my desk. To avoid distractions, I don't check e-mail, take a shower, or change my clothes before writing—I literally get up and start to write. The start and end times shift somewhat, but I spend around 2 hours writing each weekday. I'm not a morning person, but mornings work well for writing. I can get some writing out of the way before getting wrapped up in checking my mail and meeting students and colleagues who drop by the office.

Most people use a wasteful, unproductive strategy called *binge writing* (Kellogg, 1994). After intending to write, procrastinating, and feeling guilty and anxious about procrastinating, binge writers finally devote a Saturday to nothing but writing. This creates some text and alleviates the guilt, and the binge-writing cycle begins anew. Binge writers spend more time feeling guilty and anxious about not writing than schedule followers spend writing. When you follow a schedule, you no longer worry about not writing, complain about not finding time to write, or indulge in fantasies about how much you'll write over the summer. Instead, you write during your allotted times and then forget about it. We have better things to worry about than writing. I worry about whether I drink too much coffee or whether my dog drinks from the fetid backyard pond, but I don't worry about finding time to write this book: I know that I'll do it tomorrow at 8:00 a.m.

When confronted with their fruitless ways, binge writers often proffer a self-defeating dispositional attribution: "I'm just not the kind of person who's good at making a schedule and sticking to it." This is nonsense, of course. People like dispositional explanations when they don't want to change (Jellison, 1993). People who claim that they're "not the scheduling kind of person" are masterly schedulers at other times: They always teach at the same time, go to bed at the same time, watch their favorite TV shows at the same time, and so on. I've met people who jogged at the same daily time, regardless of snow or rain, but claimed that they didn't have the willpower to stick to a daily writing schedule. Don't quit before you start—making a schedule is the secret to productive writing. If you don't plan to make a schedule, gently close this book, clean it so it looks brand new, and give it as a gift to a friend who wants to be a better writer.

You must ruthlessly defend your writing time. Remember, you're *allocating* time to write, not finding time to write. You decided that this time is your time to write. Your writing time is not the time to meet with colleagues, students, or graduate advisors; it isn't the time to grade papers or develop lectures; and it certainly isn't the time to check e-mail, read the newspaper, or catch the weather report. Close your Internet access, turn off your phone, and shut the door. (I used to hang a "Do Not Disturb" sign on my office door, but people interpreted this as "His door is closed, but he wants me to know he's in there. I'll knock.")

Be forewarned that other people will not respect your commitment to your writing time. Well-intentioned intruders will want to schedule meetings with you, and they won't understand why you say no. They'll resent your inflexibility, call you rigid, and think that there's some deeper reason why you won't meet with them. For me, a common problem is that graduate students want to hold committee meetings at 9:00 a.m.—the time is convenient for them, but it's during my writing time. Likewise, I've been on some service committees in which the only time the whole group could meet was during my scheduled writing time.

How can you handle well-intentioned intruders? Just say no—that phrase might not keep you drug free, Nancy Reagan to the contrary, but it works for protecting your writing time. You have two good reasons for saying no. First, only bad writers will hold your refusal against you. I haven't met a serious writer who didn't respect my commitment to my writing time. They might be displeased that I can't meet at their preferred time, but they appreciate that scheduling is the only way to write a lot. (These people also refuse to meet with me during their scheduled writing times.) The people who grumble and whine are the unproductive writers. Don't get dragged into their bad habits. Second, the people who are happy to intrude on your writing time would never ask to intrude on your teaching time, your time that you spend with your family, or your sleeping time. They simply see your writing time as less important. As an academic psychologist, you're a professional writer, just as you're a professional teacher. Treat your scheduled writing time like your scheduled teaching time. So say no to well-intentioned intruders, and explain why you can't (not *won't*, but *can't*) break your committed writing time. If you feel bad about saying no, then lie. If you feel bad about lying, then use the obscurantism you learned in grad school: Claim a "recurring intractable obligation" or a "previously encumbered temporal placement."

Always write during your scheduled time, but don't be dogmatic about writing only within this time. It's great if you keep writing after the period is over or if you do some writing on a nonwriting day—I call this *windfall writing*. Once you harness the terrible power of habit, it'll be easier for you to sit down and write. Beware, however, of the temptation to usurp your writing schedule with windfall writing. It doesn't matter how much you wrote over spring break—you committed to your scheduled time, and you're going to stick to it. If you find yourself saying absurdities like "I wrote a lot over the weekend, so I'll skip my scheduled period on Monday," this book can help: Close it, hold it between the thumb and index finger of your nondominant hand, and wave it menacingly in front of your face.

Perhaps you're surprised by the notion of scheduling. "Is that really the trick?" you ask. "Isn't there another way to write a lot?" Nope—making a schedule and sticking to it is the only way. There is no other way to write a lot. After exhaustively researching the work habits of successful writers, Ralph Keyes (2003), a professional writer, noted that "the simple fact of sitting down to write day after day is what makes writers productive" (p. 49). If you allot 4 hours a week for writing, you will be surprised at how much you will write. By *surprised*, I mean *astonished*; and by *astonished*, I mean *dumbfounded and incoherent*. You'll find yourself committing unthinkable perversions, like finishing grant proposals early. You'll get an invitation to revise and resubmit a paper, and you'll do it within a week.

You'll be afraid to talk with friends in your department about writing out of the fear that they'll think, "You're not one of us anymore"—and they'll be right.

SPECIOUS BARRIER 2

"I need to do some more analyses first," aka, "I need to read a few more articles."

This specious barrier, perhaps the most insidious of all, has wreaked a lot of havoc. At first, this barrier seems reasonable. "After all," you might say, "you can't write a journal article without doing statistics or reading a lot of articles." True, but I've met some unproductive writers who chant this specious barrier like a mantra. Their colleagues respect them at first, believing them to be perfectionists or obsessive data analysts. But they never write much, and they never do those analyses, either. Binge writers are also binge readers and binge statisticians. The bad habits that keep them from writing also keep them from doing the *prewriting* (Kellogg, 1994), the reading, outlining, idea generation, and data analysis necessary for generating text. Like all specious barriers, this one doesn't withstand a close look.

It's easy to pull away this creaky crutch: Do whatever you need to do during your allotted writing time. Need to crunch some more statistics? Do it during your scheduled time. Need to read some articles? Do it during your scheduled time. Need to review page proofs? Do it during your scheduled time. Need to read a book about writing to get advice? You know when to do it. Writing is more than typing words: Any action that is instrumental in completing a writing project counts as writing. When writing journal articles, for example, I often spend a few consecutive writing periods working on the analyses. Sometimes I spend a whole writing period on ignominious aspects of writing, like reviewing a journal's submission guidelines, making figures and tables, or checking page proofs.

This is another reason why scheduling time to write is the only way to write a lot. Professional writing involves a lot of components: extensive literature reviews, careful analyses, and precisely worded descriptions of research methods. We will never "find the time" to retrieve and read all of the necessary articles, just as we'll never "find the time" to write a review of those articles. Use your scheduled writing time to do it. You'll no longer feel stressed about finding time to read those papers or do those analyses, because you know when you'll do it.

SPECIOUS BARRIER 3

"To write a lot, I need a new computer" (see also "a laser printer," "a nice chair," "a better desk").

Of the specious barriers, this is the most desperate. I'm not sure that people really believe this one—unlike the other specious barriers, this may be a mere excuse. A personal story might dispel this barrier. When I started writing seriously during graduate school, I bought an ancient computer from a fellow student's boyfriend. This computer was prehistoric even by 1996 standards: no mouse, no Windows, just a keyboard and WordPerfect 5.0 for DOS. When the computer died, taking some of my files with it to its grave, I bought a portable computer that I typed into the ground. I'm writing this book on a slow, tottering Toshiba laptop that I bought back in 2001—in computer years, my laptop is collecting Social Security.

For nearly 8 years, I used a metal folding chair as my official writing chair. When the folding chair retired, I replaced it with a more stylish but equally hard vintage Eames fiberglass chair. It's a simple chair: It lacks upholstery and padding, and I can't adjust the height or make it tilt. For the curious, Figure 2.1 shows where I wrote this book. There's a big, simple desk (note the lack of drawers, keyboard trays, fancy hanging-file systems, and so on) with a laser printer and a coaster for my coffee. Before I splurged on this Blu Dot desk, I had a $10 particleboard folding table, which in a nod to fashion I covered with a $4 tablecloth. I wrote most of my book about interest (Silvia, 2006) and around 20 journal articles sitting on my folding chair in front of that folding table.

Unproductive writers often bemoan the lack of "their own space" to write. I'm not sympathetic to this creaky excuse. I've never had my own room as a home office or private writing space. In a string of small apartments and houses, I wrote on a small table in the living room, in my bedroom, in the guest bedroom, in

FIGURE 2.1. Where I wrote this book.

the master bedroom, and even (briefly) in a bathroom. I wrote this book in the guest bedroom in my house. Even now, after writing all those books and articles and after buying a house, I still don't have my own space at home to write. But I don't need it—there's always a free bathroom.

I've heard a surprising number of binge writers complain about printers as barriers to writing. "If only I had a laser printer at home," they complain, with wistful yearning in their voices. They don't realize that you can't print articles like you print money—a printer only outputs what you sat down and wrote. I love my laser printer, and serious writers should buy a good one, but they're inessential. When T. Shelley Duval and I wrote our book about self-awareness (Duval & Silvia, 2001), I had a Stone Age inkjet, and he didn't have a printer. It takes a long time to print a book on an inkjet printer; we eventually printed our drafts in cyan and maroon when the black ink ran out.

When unproductive writers complain that they don't have fast Internet access at home, I congratulate them on their sound judgment. A close look at Figure 2.1 shows that there's no Internet cable plugged into the computer. My wife has fast Internet access in her home office, but I don't have anything. It's a distraction. Writing time is for writing, not for checking e-mail, reading the news, or browsing the latest issues of journals. Sometimes I think it would be nice to download articles while writing, but I can do that at the office. The best kind of self-control is to avoid situations that require self-control.

"In order to write," wrote William Saroyan (1952), "all a man needs is paper and a pencil" (p. 42). Equipment will never help you write a lot; only making a schedule and sticking to it will make you a productive writer. If you won't take my word for it, consider a recent interview with Bill Stumpf. A legend in the world of furniture design, Stumpf designs products for the Herman Miller Company, a leader in high-end office furniture. Stumpf is best known for codesigning the Aeron chair, perhaps the coolest office chair ever made. But as a writer of books himself (Stumpf, 2000), he knows that furniture can only do so much. "I'm not sure there is a direct correlation between a piece of furniture and productivity," he said, adding, "I'm sure Herman Miller wouldn't want to hear me say that" (Grawe, 2005, p. 77).

SPECIOUS BARRIER 4

"I'm waiting until I feel like it," aka "I write best when I'm inspired to write."

This final specious barrier is the most comical and irrational. I hear this one a lot from writers who, for whatever incomprehensible reason, resist making a writing schedule. "My best work comes when I'm inspired," they say. "It's no use trying to write when I'm not in the mood. I need to *feel* like writing." It's funny when thwarted writers say this. It's like cigarette addicts defending cigarettes by saying that smoking relaxes them, even though nicotine withdrawal causes the feelings of tension in the first place (Parrott, 1999). When struggling writers defend their unwillingness to make a schedule, they're sticking up for the cause of their struggles. If you believe that you should write only when you feel like writing, ask yourself some simple questions: How has this strategy worked so far? Are you happy with how much you write? Do you feel stressed about finding time to write or about completing half-finished projects? Do you sacrifice your evenings and weekends for writing?

It's easy to demolish this specious barrier: Research has shown that waiting for inspiration doesn't work. Boice (1990, pp. 79–81) conducted a study with profound implications for every binge writer who waits for inspiration. He gathered a sample of college professors who struggled with writing, and he randomly assigned them to use different writing strategies. People in an abstinence condition were forbidden from all nonemergency writing; people in a spontaneous condition scheduled 50 writing sessions but wrote only when they felt inspired; and people in a contingency management condition scheduled 50 writing sessions and were forced to write during each session. (They had to send a check to a disliked organization if they didn't do their writing.) The dependent variables were the number of pages written per day and the number of creative ideas per day. Figure 2.2 shows what Boice found. First, people in the contingency management condition wrote *a lot*: They wrote 3.5 times as many pages as people in the spontaneous condition and 16 times as much as those in the abstinence condition. People who wrote "when they felt like it" were barely more productive than people told not to write at all—inspiration is overrated. Second, forcing people to write enhanced their creative ideas for writing. The typical number of days between creative ideas was merely 1 day for people who were forced to write; it was 2 days for people in the spontaneous condition and 5 days for people in the abstinence condition. Writing breeds good ideas for writing.

Some kinds of writing are so unpleasant that no normal person will ever feel like doing them. What kind of person feels enthusiastic about writing a grant

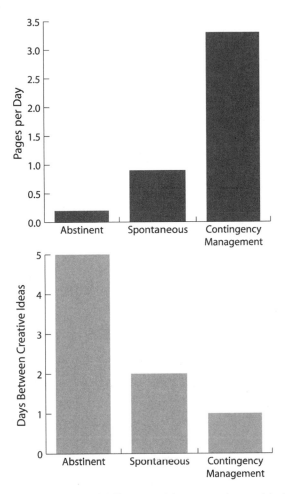

FIGURE 2.2. Effects of different writing strategies on (a) the number of pages written per day and (b) the modal number of days between creative writing ideas. Data are from Boice (1990, p. 80).

proposal? Who wakes up in the morning with an urge to write about "Specific Aims" and "Consortium/Contractual Arrangements?" Writing a grant proposal is like doing your taxes, except that you can't pay your accountant to do it for you. If you have moods where you're gripped by a desire to read the Department of Health and Human Services *Grants.gov Application Guide SF424 (R&R)*, then you don't need this book. If you're like everyone else, though, you'll need more than "feeling like it" to finish a grant proposal.

Struggling writers who "wait for inspiration" should get off their high horse and join the unwashed masses of real academic writers. The ancient Greeks assigned muses for poetry, music, and tragedy, but they didn't mention a muse for journal articles written in APA style. As academics, we're not creating high literature. We don't have fans lurking outside the conference hotel hoping for our autographs on recent issues of the *Personality and Social Psychology Bulletin*. We do technical, professional writing. Some kinds of academic writing are more relaxed—like textbooks, or perhaps this book—but even those kinds of writing boil down to imparting useful information to your readers. Our writing is important because it's practical, clear, and idea driven.

Ralph Keyes (2003) has shown that great novelists and poets—people who we think *should* wait for inspiration—reject the notion of writing when inspired. The prolific Anthony Trollope (1883/1999) wrote that there are those . . . who think that the man who works with his imagination should allow himself to wait till— inspiration moves him. When I have heard such doctrine preached, I have hardly been able to repress my scorn. To me it would not be more absurd if the shoemaker were to wait for inspiration, or the tallow-chandler for the divine moment of melting. . . . I was once told that the surest aid to the writing of a book was a piece of cobbler's wax on my chair. I certainly believe in the cobbler's wax much more than the inspiration. (p. 121)

How do these great writers write instead? Guess. Successful professional writers, regardless of whether they're writing novels, nonfiction, poetry, or drama, are prolific because they write regularly, usually every day. They reject the idea that they must be in the mood to write. As Keyes (2003) put it, "Serious writers *write*, inspired or not. Over time they discover that routine is a better friend to them than inspiration" (p. 49). One might say that they make a schedule and stick to it.

CONCLUSIONS

This chapter has cast a cold, critical eye on some common barriers to writing. We've all indulged in these comfort blankets, but it's hard to type when you're wrapped in a blanket. If you still cling to any of these specious barriers, reread this chapter until you have been indoctrinated into the glorious wonders of scheduling. This book cannot help you unless you accept the principle of scheduling, because the only way to write a lot is to write regularly, regardless of whether you feel like writing. Once you have developed a writing schedule, read the next chapter. It describes simple motivational tools for sticking to your schedule and for writing more efficiently.

3

Motivational Tools

The previous chapter demolished some false reasons for not writing. Its message was clear: Write according to a schedule. Schedules are why prolific writers are so prolific, and they are how anyone can write a lot. But perhaps you're not getting much done during your scheduled time: You sit down, coffee and computer at hand, but you're not sure what to write. Reformed binge writers usually don't know how to manage their writing time. Because they used to be driven by deadlines and guilt, they lack experience in setting goals, managing several writing projects at once, and sticking to their schedule. This chapter describes some tools for enhancing your motivation and your writing productivity. These tools presuppose that you're writing according to a schedule. If you haven't picked a schedule and committed to it yet, then you can add binge stubbornness to your bingeing repertoire.

SETTING GOALS

Like businesspeople, academics enjoy talking about goals. Some academics are so enamored of goals, initiatives, and strategic plans that they become deans and provosts. Goals deserve the attention they get. Clear goals are directly motivating—they enable people to plan, carry out instrumental actions, and feel proud when the goal has been accomplished (Bandura, 1997). Without clear goals, people's actions are diffuse and undirected (Lewin, 1935). To write a lot, you need to clarify your writing goals. This isn't as easy as it sounds; people's plans often go awry because of inadequate goal setting. Developing the right kinds of goals will make you a more efficient writer.

So how do you set good goals? The first step is to realize that goal setting is part of the process of writing. It's a good idea to devote a writing session to developing and clarifying your writing goals; I usually do this once a month. Planning is part of writing, so people who write a lot also plan a lot. The second step is to list your *project goals*—these goals are the individual projects that need to be written. Examples include revising and resubmitting a paper, starting a new manuscript, writing an invited chapter for an edited book, reviving that half-done paper you started last year, developing a grant proposal, and writing a book.

What do *you* want to write? When reformed binge writers first set writing goals, one project always leaps out—usually the dreaded project they had been avoiding for the past 3 months. Certainly write that goal down, but don't stop there. What else would you like to write during the next few months? Is there a grant proposal deadline on the horizon? Does your file cabinet have any unpublished experiments that deserve a good peer-reviewed home? Is there a review article that you always meant to write? Put down this book, get some paper, and make a sprawling, discursive list of your project goals.

After you settle on a list of project goals—and it might be a long list—you need to write these goals down. It's a waste of your writing time to rehash the planning process. Get a whiteboard or bulletin board, put it near your writing space, and proudly display your list of goals. A binge writer would feel anxious when confronted with this long list of projects, but you have a schedule. Binge writers ask, "Will I get all this done?"; disciplined writers idly wonder how many weeks it will take to write everything on the list. It's gratifying to cross a project goal off the list. You can use happy-face stickers if that's more your style.

The third step is to set a concrete goal for each day of writing. When you sit down during your writing time to work toward a project goal, you need to break the goal into smaller units. "Resubmit that paper" is fine as a project goal, but it's too broad to be useful when you sit down to write. When you start your writing period, take a couple of moments to think about what you want to accomplish that day. "Write that paper" is too general; you need a concrete goal for that day. Here are some examples of concrete daily goals:

- Write at least 200 words.
- Print the first draft I finished yesterday, read it, and revise it.
- Make a new list of project goals and write them on my whiteboard.
- Write the first three paragraphs of the general discussion.
- Add missing references and then reconcile the citations and references.
- Reread chapters 22 and 24 from Zinsser (2001) to recharge my writing batteries.
- Finish the "Setting Goals" section that I started yesterday.
- Brainstorm and then make an outline for a new manuscript.
- Reread the reviewers' comments of my paper and make a list of things to change.
- Correct the page proofs and mail them back.

Some people are surprised by goals that refer to numbers of words or paragraphs. Remember, these are *concrete* goals. It's hard to get a foothold into an abstract goal like "revise and resubmit that paper," but it's easy to understand how to write at least 200 words—you sit down and type. The irrepressible Anthony Trollope, writing with watch at hand, had the concrete goal of 250 words every 15 minutes (Trollope, 1883/1999). Get in the habit of setting specific, focused, concrete goals for each writing day. They'll prevent confusion about what to do and how to do it.

SETTING PRIORITIES

By now, you have a list of project goals. Of all of these projects, what should you write first? I asked my colleagues who write a lot how they set writing priorities. Here's a sample list—it's a rough average between my own priorities and the typical set of priorities. Use it as an example and write down your own priorities, perhaps next to your list of project goals.

1. *Checking page proofs and copyedited manuscripts.* This appears as nearly everyone's top writing priority, and for good reasons. Checking proofs is the final stage in the process of publishing, and unlike much of the world of academic writing, there's a firm deadline. Publishers need you to review page proofs and copyedited manuscripts fast, usually within 48 hours. After all the months (or years) spent collecting the data and writing the manuscript, why would you hold up your own paper? Do this fast.

2. *Finishing projects with deadlines.* Most writing tasks lack deadlines, so projects that have a due date should receive priority over those that don't. Projects with deadlines include invited book chapters, grant proposals, and administrative writing. Some of these deadlines are firm—most grant agencies won't consider proposals that are a mere day late—

and others are mushier. Personally, I don't have this as a priority category, because I don't rub against deadlines like I used to. If you follow a writing schedule, you'll finish things early. A binge writer's biggest motivator, deadlines are nearly irrelevant to disciplined, scheduled writers.

3. *Revising manuscripts to resubmit to a journal.* Most manuscripts get rejected. If you have the good fortune to be asked to resubmit your paper, don't squander it. Revised manuscripts are closer to publication than new manuscripts, so they should receive higher priority.

4. *Reviewing manuscripts and grant proposals.* This is a controversial category; I found little agreement among my colleagues regarding where reviews should fall in the priority list. Some thought reviews should be a high-priority nonwriting task, one worth doing quickly but not during scheduled writing time. Others were indifferent toward reviews and tended to put them off. For what it's worth, I place reviews relatively high. The peer review process is only as good as the peers who review. The review process in psychology is too slow, and this hurts the field's scientific mission. If everyone were a faster reviewer, everyone would be a happier author. Writing reviews quickly also wins you the goodwill of editors, who are constantly exasperated by slow reviewers. The same

holds for grants: A lot is at stake with grant reviews, so they're worth doing quickly and well.

5. *Developing a new manuscript.* Published papers start with the first draft of a manuscript. Writing a manuscript from the ground up is hard for binge writers: They spread it out over months, and they do their literature reviews and data analyses in binges, too. Writing new manuscripts is relatively easy (compared with grants, books, and revised manuscripts) when you follow a schedule. Chapter 6 gives helpful tips for writing empirical papers.

6. *Doing miscellaneous writing.* This is a catch-all category for unimportant writing that still needs to be done, like a brief article for a newsletter. It helps to have some fun side projects that you can tinker with when you have a lull in your major writing projects.

Nearly everyone I surveyed mentioned that they place particular priority on writing projects involving graduate students. They might usually devote their time to a resubmission, for instance, but they'll privilege a new manuscript when a graduate student is a coauthor. This is sound advice. I also give priority to projects in which I'm a nonwriting coauthor. Ever write a first draft, send it to the second and third authors for comments and changes, and never hear back from them? It's maddening to be held up by a slow coauthor, especially when he or she doesn't have the burden of generating much text. Binge writing is bad, but binge coauthoring is worse.

Graduate students should have different writing priorities than faculty. This priority list was developed by talking with successful graduate students and recent graduates.

1. *Projects with deadlines.* Graduate school involves a lot of deadline writing, such as required papers for classes and seminars. Many students complain that their class assignments soak up writing time that could be spent on more significant projects, like a master's thesis. That's true, but deadlines are deadlines, and these papers are good practice for the real world of academic writing. Also, if you need more time to write, simply add more hours to your weekly writing schedule. Grant proposals—such as fellowships that support graduate training—also have deadlines, and they're well worth the effort.

2. *Curricular writing.* In graduate school, you'll have writing projects that define your school's degree program: typically a master's thesis, a comprehensive or qualifying paper, and a dissertation. You need to do these to graduate, so do them quickly. These projects sometimes yield publishable products, so many students can integrate their curricular tasks with real professional writing.

3. *Professional publications.* Scientific research counts only if it's published in an accessible, peer-reviewed outlet. It's great that you finished your thesis and that your committee liked it, but the world's scientists need to be able to access it and scrutinize it. Strong theses and dissertations should be submitted to professional journals. Moreover, you should aspire to publish more than your thesis and dissertation. Take every opportunity to get involved in research projects and writing projects. If you make a writing schedule, you'll be the most prolific student in your program.

4. *Other writing.* Graduate students often do a surprising amount of miscellaneous writing, like reviewing books and contributing to bulletins and newsletters. Like all writing, this writing is good practice and worth the time. But these projects are less important than peer-reviewed, archived professional publications such as journal articles and book chapters. If faced with two options, always make professional writing a higher priority.

When we talk about setting priorities, people commonly ask, "But what if I have nothing to write?" It's rare that professors have *nothing* to write. To the contrary, most faculty I know have a dark, vast backlog of unpublished data. Collecting data is easy; writing about data is hard. If you have experiments that you ran 10 years ago but never published, it'll be a while before you have nothing to write. Moreover, writing begets writing. As Boice (1990) found, people who wrote regularly had more creative ideas for writing compared with people who wrote only when they felt like it (see chap. 2). If you think you have nothing to write, spend a writing period making a new set of project goals.

Graduate students, however, can realistically find themselves without a current writing project. Perhaps you just wrapped up your thesis and have no other projects, or perhaps you just started graduate school. Fear not: You have two good options. First, get involved in an ongoing writing project. Your advisor, like most professors, probably struggles with writing and has a few stalled writing projects. Wander into his or her office and say "I've been reading some books about how to be a better writer, and one of them suggested wandering into your office and asking if I could get involved in some writing projects. If you have any manuscripts that need work or some data that need to be submitted, I'd like to help out." There's a realistic possibility that your advisor will sputter incoherently. Faculty wish that graduate students took more initiative in research and writing, so your advisor will be pleased that you want to get involved.

Another way you can deal with not having anything to write is to use your scheduled writing time for your professional development. One of the best tips I ever got in grad school was to "always make time to think." Grad school is hectic; it's easy to lose sight of your long-range goals when you're struggling to manage a lot of short-term deadlines. Having a few hours to yourself each week will give you time to read books about writing and teaching, to reflect on your research, and to think about your broader career goals.

Monitoring Progress

Most people have no idea how much—or how little— they're writing. Because they view themselves in a flattering, self-enhancing light, most people think that they're writing more often and more efficiently than they are. To write a lot, you need to take a cold, accurate look at your writing by monitoring your writing progress. Research on self-regulation shows that it isn't enough to set a goal and make it a priority: People must monitor their progress toward the goal (Carver & Scheier, 1998; Duval & Silvia, 2001).

Monitoring your writing progress has many good motivational effects. First, watching your progress keeps your goals salient, which prevents them from slipping away. Many people struggle with managing all the things they have to write. Monitoring your writing will keep you focused on your ongoing project. Second, merely monitoring your behavior will help you sit down and write. Behavioral research shows that self-observation alone can cause the desired behaviors (see Korotitsch & Nelson-Gray, 1999). For example, people who want to save money should keep track of their daily expenses, because the mere tracking of their spending will make them spend less. Likewise, people who want to write regularly should keep track of whether they sat down and wrote: Typing a big ugly zero in a spreadsheet when you miss a writing period is oddly motivating. Finally, monitoring your writing will help you set better goals. After a while, you'll have enough data on yourself to make realistic estimates of how long it will take to write something. Better goal setting, in turn, leads to more productive writing.

People who write a lot typically do some kind of monitoring. There are different ways to do this; in this section I describe how I monitor my writing. When I tell people about my system they give me an odd look, as if I had just said that I make quilts out of Bernese mountain dog hair. The system sounds nerdy, obsessive, and weird, but it helps me stay focused. I have an SPSS data file called "Writing Progress.sav"; Figure 3.1 gives a screenshot of the file. I created variables for the month, date, day of the week, and year. These variables let me identify a given day. The essential variables are called *words*, *goal*, and *project*. In the *words* column, I enter the number of words I wrote that day. Any word processor will give you the number of words in your document; just get this number before you start and after you finish, and you can take the difference. Notice that this column has a lot of empty cells. As I've emphasized, writing involves many tasks, not just generating text. Some days I spend reading articles, filling out forms for a grant proposal, or rereading a

Writing Progress.sav - SPSS Data Editor

File Edit View Data Transform Analyze Graphs Utilities Add-ons Window Help

173

	month	date	day	words	goal	project	comments	year	year
173	June	14.00	Tuesday		Met	Emotion Concepts Paper		2005	
174	June	15.00	Wednesda		Met	Trait Curiosity JPA Paper		2005	
175	June	16.00	Thursday	137.00	Met	Emotion Concepts Paper		2005	
176	June	17.00	Friday	321.00	Met	SAI C3, Emotion Concepts Paper		2005	
177	June	18.00	Saturday	305.00	Met	SAI C3		2005	
178	June	19.00	Sunday		Met	ESM Grant		2005	
179	June	20.00	Monday	390.00	Met	SAI C3		2005	
180	June	21.00	Tuesday	1154.00	Met	SAI C3		2005	
181	June	22.00	Wednesda	363.00	Met	JPSP Revisions		2005	
182	June	23.00	Thursday		Met	SAI C3		2005	
183	June	24.00	Friday		Met	ESM Grant		2005	
184	June	25.00	Saturday		Met	SAI C3		2005	
185	June	26.00	Sunday		Met	SAI C3		2005	
186	June	27.00	Monday		Met	ESM Grant		2005	
187	June	28.00	Tuesday		Met	ESM Grant		2005	
188	June	29.00	Wednesda		Met	Reactance Revision		2005	
189	June	30.00	Thursday	1488.00	Met	Reactance Revision, Submitted)		2005	
190	July	1.00	Friday		Met	SAI C3		2005	
191	July	2.00	Saturday	354.00	Met	SAI C3		2005	
192	July	3.00	Sunday	373.00	Met	SAI C3		2005	
193	July	4.00	Monday		Met	SAI C3		2005	
194	July	5.00	Tuesday		Unmet			2005	
195	July	6.00	Wednesda	433.00	Met	JSCP Revisions		2005	
196	July	7.00	Thursday		Met	JSCP Revisions		2005	
197	July	8.00	Friday		Met	OSA Effort Revisions		2005	
198	July	9.00	Saturday		Met	OSA Effort Revisions		2005	
199	July	10.00	Sunday		Met	OSA Effort Revisions		2005	
200	July	11.00	Monday		Met	SAI C3		2005	
201	July	12.00	Tuesday		Met	JSCP Paper		2005	
202	July	13.00	Wednesda		Met	JSCP Paper		2005	
203	July	14.00	Thursday		Met	Sam's paper		2005	

Data View Variable View

SPSS Processor is ready

FIGURE 3.1. My "Writing Progress.sav" file as an example of how you can monitor your writing.

41

manuscript that needs to be resubmitted. I leave the cell blank for these days. The purpose of the *goal* column is to mark whether I met my writing goal for that day. My personal goal is simply to sit down and do something that furthers my project goal, so I score this variable as {0 = Unmet, 1 = Met}. I did pretty well during the period shown in Figure 3.1; I failed to meet my goal on July 5, but I met it on the other days. The *project* column describes the project goal I worked on that day. Recording the project lets you see how long it took to finish a project. Sometimes it feels like a project drags on forever, but it may have been briefer than you remember.

Binge writers who are still clinging to specious barriers might say "But I don't have SPSS," or even "But I use SAS!" Any statistics or spreadsheet program will do, and I'm sure you have access to lined notebook paper and pencils. The tracking is the key, not the technology. But a statistics program lets you mine your writing data. If you're a statistics fan—and who isn't?—you'll love the ability to get statistics about your writing. I wrote a short SPSS syntax file that computes some descriptive statistics and histograms. When I spent a period writing new text, I averaged 789 words per day; Figure 3.2 shows a histogram. It doesn't sound like a lot, but it adds up. Figure 3.3 plots *goal* by month; this figure shows that some months were better than others. According to my writing data, I sat down to write on 97% of my scheduled days during the past 12 months. I'm not perfect, but I'm pretty happy with

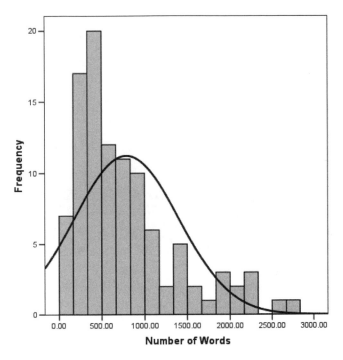

FIGURE 3.2. A histogram of the average number of words written per day over the past 12 months.

that number. Monitoring it lets me try to improve it, and I feel proud when I get 100% for the month. If you're curious, you could also plot *goal* and *words* data by day of the week. So, when people ask me how much I write, I can say I write 97% of the weekdays, and when I generate text I average 789 words per day. They might give me the Bernese-mountain-dog-quilt look, but that's okay.

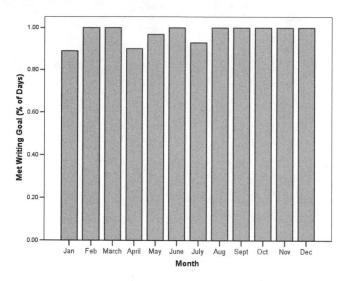

FIGURE 3.3. A histogram of the proportion of times the daily writing goal was met over the past 12 months.

Reward yourself when you finish a project goal. Self-reinforcement and contingency management are time honored ways of fostering desirable behaviors (Skinner, 1987). When you submit a paper or grant proposal, buy yourself a nice cup of coffee, a good lunch, or a vintage Heywood-Wakefield end table. Writing's rewards are delayed—it takes months to hear from journal editors and grant panels—so immediate self-rewards will sustain your motivation. Only a fool, however, rewards productive writing with skipping a scheduled writing period. Never reward writing with not writing. Rewarding writing by abandoning your schedule is like rewarding yourself for quitting smoking by having a cigarette. The writing schedule works by harnessing the awesome powers of routine and habit: Don't lose your good writing habits.

What About Writer's Block?

"Wait," you might say. "So far, this book hasn't said anything about writer's block. Sure, you can make a schedule, set goals, and monitor your progress, but what happens when you get writer's block?" I love writer's block. I love it for the same reasons I love tree spirits and talking woodland creatures—they're charming and they don't exist. When people tell me they have writer's block, I ask, "What on earth are you trying to write?" Academic writers cannot get writer's block. Don't confuse yourself with your friends teaching creative writing in the fine arts department. You're not crafting a deep narrative or composing metaphors that expose mysteries of the human heart. The subtlety of your analysis of variance will not move readers to tears, although the tediousness of it might. People will not photocopy your reference list and pass it out to friends whom they wish to inspire. Novelists and poets are the landscape artists and portrait painters; academic writers are the people with big paint sprayers who repaint your basement.

Writer's block is a good example of a dispositional fallacy: A description of behavior can't also explain the described behavior. Writer's block is nothing more

than the behavior of not writing. Saying that you can't write because of writer's block is merely saying that you can't write because you aren't writing. It's trivial. The cure for writer's block—if you can cure a specious affliction—is writing. Recall Boice's (1990) experiment described in chapter 2. In that study, struggling writers wrote a lot when they simply followed a schedule—that's all it took. In contrast, struggling writers who waited until they "felt like it" wrote almost nothing. If you really have writer's block, you can (a) stop working on your Collected Poems and get back to writing your journal article, (b) persuade the tree spirits and talking woodland creatures to write your general discussion for you, or (c) redevelop your writing schedule and recommit to sticking to it.

Just as aliens abduct only people who believe in alien abductions, writer's block strikes only writers who believe in it. One of the great mysteries of the writing schedule system—a spooky mystery, in fact—is that scheduled writers don't get writer's block, whatever that is. Prolific writers follow their writing schedule regardless of whether they feel like writing. Some days they don't write much—writing is a grim business, after all—but they're nevertheless sitting and writing, oblivious to the otherworldly halo hovering above their house.

CONCLUSIONS

This chapter has described motivational tools that will make you a more productive writer. After you've committed to a writing schedule, you need to make a list of your project goals and write them down. When you sit down to write, spend a minute thinking about what you want to do that day. Setting priorities among your project goals will take the stress out of managing several projects at once. And monitoring your writing will keep you focused on your goals, motivate you not to miss a day, inform you about how well you're doing, and give you hard facts that you can show to your binge-writing colleagues who are doubters and unbelievers. Anyone who combines the tips in this chapter with a regular schedule will write a lot.

4

Starting Your Own Agraphia Group

Complaining is an academic's birthright. The art of complaining develops early, when undergraduates complain about their professors, their textbooks, and the cosmic unfairness of 9:00 a.m. Friday classes. In graduate school, complaining approaches professional levels—students are aggrieved by the tediousness of statistics classes, the imperiousness of their graduate advisors, and the omnipresent half-written dissertation. And, of course, professional faculty raise complaining to a refined, elegant art, particularly when provosts or parking permits are involved.

Sometimes these complaints involve writing. Professors and graduate students both like to complain about writing: how hard it is to finish the dissertation, how they might not finish the grant proposal before the deadline, how they didn't write as much during spring break as they had hoped. Complaining about writing is usually bad, especially when it involves the specious barriers described in chapter 2. When people sit around and talk about what they could accomplish if only they could find time to write or get a new computer, they're colluding to maintain their useless, wasteful, binge-writing habits. But can we harness the proud academic tradition of complaining for the sake of good, not evil? Can we use our atavistic academic instinct toward collective whining to help us write a lot?

This chapter describes how you can create your own *agraphia group*, a type of support group for people who want to write faster and better. It uses principles of motivation, goal setting, and social support to help people maintain good writing habits. If you followed the tips in chapters 2 and 3, then you have a writing schedule, a list of project goals, and a set of writing priorities. A writing group will reinforce these good habits and keep you from slipping back into the darkness of binge writing.

THE AGRAPHIA MODEL

The psychology department at University of North Carolina at Greensboro (UNCG), like psychology departments everywhere, has a lot of faculty members who wish they could write more productively. A few years ago, Cheryl Logan, a friend of mine in the department, had the idea of creating a weekly writer's group. We thought it would be fun to organize the group around research on goal setting, which offers practical tips for sustaining optimal motivation (e.g., Bandura,

1997). I suggested calling the group the Trollope Society in honor of the Victorian novelist Anthony Trollope. Trollope wrote 63 books; most were two- or three-volume works. Psychologists can learn a lot from Trollope. He wrote most of his books, including the classic six-novel series *Chronicles of Barsetshire*, while working full time at the post office (Pope-Hennessy, 1971). To accomplish this, he wrote each morning from 5:30 until breakfast. As he remarked in his autobiography, "Three hours a day will produce as much as a man ought to write" (Trollope, 1883/1999, p. 271).

Trollope was a great writer, but "the Trollope Society" was a bad name. Cheryl suggested *agraphia*—the pathologic loss of the ability to write—which nicely captured how most of us felt about writing. We rustled up some faculty, and the Agraphia Group was born. The purpose of the UNCG Agraphia Group is to give people a chance to talk about ongoing writing projects, to get others' ideas and insights about writing challenges, and to help each other set reasonable goals. We haven't conducted a formal program evaluation, so we lack hard data that support our agraphia model. Nevertheless, we've met regularly for several years, and we believe that it helps. We can also boast of independent replications of the agraphia model—friends at other universities heard about our success and started their own groups. A successful agraphia group has five components.

Component 1: Set Concrete, Short-Term Goals and Monitor the Group's Progress

Motivation research shows that *proximal goal setting* enhances motivation (Bandura, 1997). When people set concrete, short-term goals, they can see ways of achieving the goals and monitor how quickly they are moving toward their goals. At each agraphia meeting, the members should set goals that they'll commit to completing before the next meeting. These goals resemble the goals described in chapter 3: They must be specific. Goals like "think about my paper" should get struck down by the group; goals like "make an outline for my paper," "write the general discussion," "write at least 1,000 words on my book," and "call the NIMH program officer to discuss my grant proposal" should be encouraged. Trying to write isn't writing—don't let a group member get away with goals like "try to make an outline" or "try to write 100 words."

As we saw in chapter 3, people must monitor their goal progress. We bring the Folder of Goals to each meeting, and each person says what he or she plans to do before the next meeting. We write down each person's concrete goals and keep them in the folder. At the start of the next meeting, we recite the past week's goals and say whether or not we met them. Figure 4.1 shows a recent sheet of goals. Our system prevents people from wriggling out of their goals or having false memories about what they said the week before.

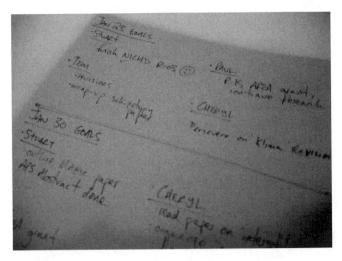

FIGURE 4.1. An example of our agraphia group's goals. The names have been left alone to expose the guilty.

An agraphia group should meet every week or every other week. Beyond 2 weeks, people's goals become too abstract and long range. We have a set of core members who meet weekly. Some members can make it only every other week, so they set bigger goals than the rest of us.

Component 2: Stick to Writing Goals, Not Other Professional Goals

Professors have a lot of obligations. It's easy for an agraphia meeting to degenerate into complaining about service committees, teaching, or wayward grad students. Avoid this. Many of our meetings are brief:

We break out the prior week's goals, check off which were met and unmet, and set new goals. It might take only a few minutes per person. If we have extra time, we usually chat about challenges that members are facing, such as approaching a book publisher regarding a contract, motivating an agraphic graduate student, or developing a grant proposal for the first time.

When getting your own agraphia group off the ground, consider having the group read books about writing. You can discuss the books after reviewing and setting goals. This book is a natural choice; in the back of this book, you'll find a list of other books worth reading and discussing. If group members struggle with style, pick *On Writing Well* (Zinsser, 2001) and *Junk English* (Smith, 2001). If the group struggles with motivation, turn to *The Writer's Book of Hope* (Keyes, 2003), *Professors as Writers* (Boice, 1990), and Stephen King's *On Writing* (2000).

Component 3: Big Carrots Can Double as Sticks

The agraphia group should reinforce good writing habits with informal social rewards. It's a big deal when a group member submits a grant proposal or sends a manuscript to a journal. If the agraphia members suffer from caffeine dependency, you can reinforce writing behavior by paying for another member's coffee. The small carrots of social life are a big part of an agraphia group's success. But support groups shouldn't be unconditionally supportive. If someone consistently fails to meet his or her writing goals, the group needs to intervene. The group is not a forum for indulging in specious barriers or for justifying a consistently bad level of writing. It's rare that a member is completely stuck—those people never come to the meetings in the first place—but the group should be ready to confront someone who consistently fails to meet his or her goals. A good way to do this is to ask the person about his or her writing schedule. This question usually reveals that the person hasn't been following a schedule. Then goad the wayward group member into forming a more realistic schedule and pressure him or her into committing to it for the next week. Do this every week until the person breaks down and writes. If that method doesn't work, consider using psychology's time-honored method of motivating behavior with electric shocks.

Component 4: Have Different Groups for Faculty and Students

The UNCG Agraphia Group is for faculty members only; we don't invite graduate students to attend. It sounds unfair, but there are good reasons why faculty and graduate students should have different groups. Faculty and students have different writing priorities (see chap. 3), and they face different struggles and different challenges. Graduate students often feel intimidated in a large group of faculty, erroneously believing that their writing goals (e.g., finishing a master's

55

thesis) are less important than the professors' goals. When professors are alone, they can speak candidly about their struggles with mentoring students as writers and about stalled projects involving students. When students are alone, they can speak candidly about struggles with class projects and with writing projects involving their advisors.

If you're a graduate student, many of your friends are probably other students in your cohort. You're facing the same writing challenges—theses, dissertations—at the same time, so an agraphia group is a natural way to support each other's writing. Start a students-only writing group, and keep it a secret from your advisor—he or she might want to join.

Component 5 (Optional): Drink Coffee

Because of the profound caffeine addiction of its members, the UNCG Agraphia Group meets at a coffee shop next to the department. Although coffee is an important part of our group, it doesn't seem to affect the other agraphia groups. Tea—or perhaps even water—may work equally well.

CONCLUSIONS

By now, it's clear to psychologists why an agraphia group helps people write a lot. Social psychologists realize that the group is a constructive source of social pressure. People who are binge writing will feel pressured by the scheduled writers to make a schedule and

stick to it. Behavioral psychologists notice that the group provides positive reinforcement for the desired behavior and punishment for not behaving properly. Clinical psychologists recognize that the group can provide insights and suggestions to people struggling to change their unproductive ways. Cognitive psychologists point out that analyzing successes and failures enables people to evaluate their action strategies. Developmental psychologists realize that they can get away from the children shrieking in the lab and have a moment of peace in the coffee shop. Form an agraphia group with some friends in your department—it will make writing more fun.

5

A Brief Foray Into Style

Our academic journals radiate bad writing—I store my journals on the shelf farthest from my desk to avoid the fallout. But if you talk with the authors of these disastrously written articles, you'll find that they're enthusiastic about their work. Their spoken descriptions are often clear, lively, and interesting. What went wrong? This book is about writing a lot, not about writing well, but you should take the time to learn the principles of strong writing. People can write a lot after a mere week if they commit to following a schedule, but it takes much longer to learn how to write well—all the more reason to start now. This chapter provides a handful of tips for improving the quality of your writing.

DIAGNOSING THE PROBLEM

Academic writers are bad writers for three reasons. First, they want to sound smart. "If the water is dark," goes a German aphorism, "the lake must be deep."

Instead of using good words like *smart*, they choose *sophisticated* or *erudite*. I ought to have said, "Bodies of water characterized by minimal transparency are likely to possess significantly high values on the depth dimension ($p < .05$)." Second, academic writers never learned how to write well. Their role models during graduate school were probably bad writers, and their role models in the journals set the Geiger counters clicking. Finally, most academics don't spend enough time writing to become good writers. As with any other skill, writing skill comes from many hours of deliberate practice (Ericsson, Krampe, & Tesch-Römer, 1993). People must learn the rules of good writing and spend hundreds of hours practicing those rules.

To solve the first problem, you must revise your mental model of academic writing. Some readers might think you're smart if your writing is impenetrable, but you don't want that undiscerning audience. Most scientists are impressed by good ideas and interesting findings, so don't hide your ideas behind a wall of junk English. To solve the second problem, read this chapter and then buy some books about writing. At the back of this book is a list of references about style and grammar that you'll find helpful (see "Good Books About Writing"). To solve the third problem, read those books and practice their suggestions during your scheduled writing time. It won't be long before your sentences sound more like you and less like an anonymous, desiccated academic.

CHOOSE GOOD WORDS

Writing begins and ends with words. To write well, you need to choose good words. The English language has a lot of words, and many of them are short, expressive, and familiar—write with these words. Avoid trendy phrases that sound intellectual, and never use words that make you sound like an academic psychologist. Besides improving your writing, good words show respect for your many readers who learned English as a second, third, or fourth language. Foreign scholars often read articles with a dual-language dictionary at hand. If a word isn't in that dictionary, your foreign readers won't understand it. They'll blame themselves for misunderstanding your writing, but you're to blame for leaving them behind.

"But what about technical terms?" you might ask. "How can I write a paper about stimulus onset asynchrony without saying 'stimulus onset asynchrony'?" Science coins words and phrases when it needs them— these technical terms do useful work. When defined with normal words, technical terms are easy to understand. We should keep our good science words and exclude the bad words that emigrate from business, marketing, politics, and warfare: We don't need verbs like *to incentivize* or *to target*, and only window washers need adjectives like *transparent*. For coherence, use technical terms consistently. Varying terms for psychological concepts will confuse your readers:

Before: People high in neuroticism responded slower than people low in the tendency to experience aversive affective states.

After: People high in neuroticism responded slower than people low in neuroticism.

But some technical terms are terrible, so don't mindlessly write the words you see in professional journals. Developmental psychologists, content with neither *path* nor *way*, describe developmental *pathways*; in vaunted moments, these pathways are *trajectories*. Cognitive psychologists should *clarify* what *disambiguate* means. Clinical psychologists have clients who *present with* symptoms, presumably like depressed butlers carrying platters of "negative moods" and "poor sleep." And clinicians don't write manuals or follow manuals anymore; they develop and implement *manualized interventions*. Emotion psychologists, fearing their readers' ignorance of the meaning of *appraisal*, speak of *cognitive appraisals*, *subjective appraisals*, and—in case someone missed the point—*subjective cognitive appraisals*. Psychologists with interdisciplinary interests propose *biosocial* models, *psychosocial* models, *psychobiological* models, and even *biopsychosocial* models; a recent *biopsychosocialspiritual* model surpasses parochial models that are merely biopsychosocial.

Psychologists love bad words, although they call them *deficient* or *suboptimal* instead of *bad*. Psychologists like writing about *the existing literature*. Is there a nonexistent literature that I should be reading and referencing? Any psychologist who reads articles should know that our professional journals are frighteningly real. *Extant literature* is a white-collar version of the same crime. Psychologists who write about *a disconnect* between two things have become disconnected from their dictionaries, where they'll find good words like *difference, distinction, separation,* and *gap.* And some individuals, when writing individual papers on various individual topics, refer to *a person* as *an individual* and to *people* as *individuals.* These people forget that *individual* is vague: Consider "We observed an individual _____." Should the blank be filled with a noun (e.g., rabbit) or with a verb (e.g., walking)? You don't say *individual* and *individuals* when discussing research with your friends, so why be so shoddy when describing it to the vast world of science? Were you attracted to psychology because you were interested in individuals and enjoyed individuals-watching? Choose good words, like *person* and *people.* The abomination *persons* should remain the property of small-town sheriffs on the hunt for "a person or persons unknown."

Speaking of people, I stopped writing *participants* when describing my research participants. I have friends who study birds, infants, rats, and school districts; their participants are nothing like mine. I study adult humans, so *person* and *people* are good words for my Methods sections. If this decision shocks you, fear not—unlike fashion, APA style lacks police. *Participants* is a vague word, so psychologists should choose better words. Some researchers, for example, study children by collecting data from children, teachers, and parents. People in all three groups are participants, so the word is uninformative: Call them children, teachers, and parents. If you study cognitive processes in older and younger adults, why not describe your methods and results using *older adults* and *younger adults*? In the privacy of your own room, rewrite a Methods section by replacing the word *participants* with a better word. You'll feel better.

Abbreviations and acronyms are bad words. I've seen writers abbreviate short, familiar words like *anxiety* (ANX) and *depression* (DEP), add acronyms for simple phrases like *anxious arousal* (ANXAR) and *anhedonic depression* (ANDEP), and then gleefully describe the differences between ANX, ANDEP, DEP, and ANXAR. Abbreviations and acronyms are useful only when they are easier to understand than the tortuous phrases they represent. SES and ANOVA are good; ANX and DEP are bad. Some writers believe that they're reducing redundancy by replacing common phrases with abbreviations. In a book about how to write a lot, for example, they would rather repeat *WAL* than *write a lot*. Readers find rereading abbreviations more tedious than rereading real words. By not writing tortuous phrases in the first place, you'll reduce the need for abbreviations.

Delete *very, quite, basically, actually, virtually, extremely, remarkably, completely, at all*, and so forth. Basically, these quite useless words add virtually nothing at all; like weeds, they'll in fact actually smother your sentences completely. In *Junk English*, Ken Smith (2001) called these words *parasitic intensifiers*:

> Formerly strong words are being reduced to lightweights that need to be bulked up with intensifiers to regain their punch. To *offer insight* or to *oppose a position* now sound tepid unless the insight is *valuable* and the opposition *diametrical*. The intensifier drains the vigor from its host. (p. 98)

If you took to heart Strunk and White's (2000) command to "omit needless words" (p. 23) but can't tell which words are needless, parasitic intensifiers are basically begging to be totally eliminated.

WRITE STRONG SENTENCES

Now that you're self-conscious about your words—"Did I write *individuals* in my last paper?"—it's time to rethink how to write sentences. "All this time you have been writing sentences," wrote Sheridan Baker (1969), "as naturally as breathing, and perhaps with as little variation" (p. 27). By overusing a single type of sentence, bad writers sound like they're speaking in a discursive drone. English has three types of sentences: simple, compound, and complex (Baker, 1969; Hale, 1999). *Simple sentences* have only one subject–predicate pair. Academic writers scorn clear, simple sentences. It's a shame. *Compound sentences* have two clauses, and each clause can stand alone. Sometimes a conjunction connects the independent clauses;

sometimes a semicolon does the trick. Unlike simple and compound sentences, *complex sentences* contain dependent and independent clauses. Complex sentences, if written well, give your writing a crisp, controlled tone.

In egocentric moments, I believe that parallel sentences were invented for psychologists. We write about relationships, contrasts, and comparisons: people high in extraversion and people low in extraversion, the control condition and the experimental condition, what happened at Time 1 and what happened at Time 2. Good writers use parallel sentences because parallel structures easily express relationships; bad writers avoid them because they think that parallel structures are repetitive. Instead, bad writers create skewed sentences by varying their terms and sentence types:

> *Before*: People in the dual-task condition monitored a series of beeps while reading a list of words. Some other participants in a different group read only a list of words without listening for sounds ("control condition").

> *After*: People in the dual-task condition monitored a series of beeps while reading a list of words. People in the control condition read a list of words.

Some parallel sentences use a *criterion–variant structure*: They describe what is shared and then describe the variations.

> *Better*: Everyone read a list of words. People in the dual-task condition monitored a series of beeps while reading the words, and people in the control condition only read the words.

Better: Everyone viewed a set of 20 pictures. In the control condition, people merely viewed the pictures. In the evaluation condition, people rated how much they liked each picture.

Many people are estranged from the semicolon, a good but neglected friend to writers of parallel sentences. Like their dislike of jocks and the yearbook club, many writers' distrust of semicolons is a prejudice from high school. Work through this—you need semicolons. Semicolons must connect independent clauses; each part of the sentence must be able to stand alone. Unlike a period, a semicolon implies a close connection between the clauses. Unlike a comma followed by *and*, a semicolon implies a sense of balance, of weighing one and the other. Semicolons are thus ideal for coordinating two parallel sentences:

Before: At Time 1, people read the words. At Time 2, they tried to remember as many words as possible.

After: At Time 1, people read the words; at Time 2, they tried to remember as many words as possible.

Before: People in the reading condition read the words, and people in the listening condition heard a recording of the words.

After: People in the reading condition read the words; people in the listening condition heard a recording of the words.

While you're rebuilding your relationship with the semicolon, reach out and make a new friend—the dash. Good writers are addicted to dashes. Technically called *em dashes*—they're the width of a capital M—dashes enable crisp, striking sentences. Dashes have two common uses (Gordon, 2003). First, a single dash can connect a clause or phrase to the end of sentence. You've read a lot of these in this chapter:

- Our academic journals radiate bad writing—I store my journals on the shelf farthest from my desk to avoid the fallout.
- Work through this—you need semicolons.
- While you're rebuilding your relationship with the semicolon, reach out and make a new friend—the dash.

Second, two dashes can enclose a parenthetical expression. You've read these, too:

- Now that you're self-conscious about your words—"Did I write *individuals* in my last paper?"—it's time to rethink how to write sentences.
- Technically called *em dashes*—they're the width of a capital M—dashes enable crisp, striking sentences.

Try using dashes for your next Participants and Design section:

Okay: Forty-two adults participated in the experiment. There were 12 women and 30 men.

Better: Forty-two adults—12 women and 30 men—participated in the experiment.

The em dash has a lesser known cousin, the *en dash*. The width of a capital *N*, the en dash coordinates two concepts. It's a clean way of expressing *between*. Few writers use en dashes properly; they use hyphens instead, often with embarrassing results. Developmental psychologists interested in *parent-child behavior* probably don't mean that parents act like babies sometimes—they mean *parent–child*, a shorthand for "behavior between parents and children." Good writers know the difference between a *teacher–parent conference* (en dash) and a *teacher-parent conference* (hyphen). A researcher on my campus posted flyers for an "infant-parent interaction study." (Forget teen pregnancy— let's stop infant pregnancy.) Now is a good time to thank the valiant copyeditors who have silently corrected en dash errors in your published papers.

You can write strong sentences by experimenting with appositional phrases. Because the positions of phrases in a sentence imply relationships, you can eliminate words that connect and coordinate parts of the sentence.

> *Before: Counterfactual thoughts*, which are defined as thoughts about events that did not occur, demonstrate the intersection of cognition and emotion.

> *After: Counterfactual thoughts*, defined as thoughts about events that did not occur, demonstrate the intersection of cognition and emotion.

> *Better: Counterfactual thoughts*—thoughts about events that did not occur—demonstrate the intersection of cognition and emotion.

Before: The study of facial expressions is a popular area within the study of cognition and emotion, and it has settled old conflicts about the structure of emotions.

After: The study of facial expressions, a popular area within the study of cognition and emotion, has settled old conflicts about the structure of emotions.

Finally, you can diagnose weak sentences by checking for two common maladies that strike academic writing. The first, the *such that* virus, afflicts writers who fear simple sentences. To avoid writing a simple sentence, they use *such that* to connect a flabby first clause with the second clause that they meant to write. Never write *such that* again. Use your word processor's search function to stamp out this pestilence. If you find it, there are three cures: delete the clause preceding *such that*, replace *such that* with a colon or dash, or write a better sentence.

Before: We created two conditions such that people in one condition were told to be accurate and people in another condition were told to be fast.

After: People in one condition were told to be accurate; people in another condition were told to be fast. (Dropped the preceding clause, used a semicolon to create parallel clauses.)

After: We created two conditions: People in one condition were told to be accurate, and people in another condition were told be to fast. (Replaced *such that* with a colon.)

Before: People were assigned to groups such that the assignment process was random.

After: People were randomly assigned to groups. (Wrote a better sentence.)

The second malady, the *wobbly compound syndrome*, afflicts writers who erroneously believe that commas should mark pauses in speech. Our journals are battling a pandemic of wobbly compound syndrome. Some examples of casualties follow:

- Positive moods enhance creative problem solving, and broaden thinking.
- Experiment 1 demonstrated strong effects of planning on motivation, and clarified competing predictions about how planning works.

Recognize the symptoms? Know why these are wrong? Compound sentences require two independent clauses. In wobbly compounds, the second clause can't stand alone because it lacks a subject: What broadens thinking? What clarified predictions? It's easy to fix these sentences. You can add a subject to the second clause ("and *they* broaden thinking," "and *it* clarified competing predictions") or you can omit the comma ("Positive moods enhance creative problem solving and broaden thinking.")

AVOID PASSIVE, LIMP, AND WORDY PHRASES

All books about writing urge people to write in the active voice. People think actively and speak actively, so active writing captures the compelling sound of everyday thought and speech. Passive writing, by hiding the sentence's doer, strikes people as vague and evasive. Writers who want to sound smart drift toward the passive voice; they like its impersonal sound and its stereotypical association with scholarly writing. Passive writing is easy to fix. Read your writing, and circle each appearance of the infinitive *to be*. Can you think of a better verb? Nearly all verbs imply being, so you can usually replace *to be* with dynamic verbs. Change at least one third of your original uses of *to be*. With vigilance and practice, you'll write fewer passive sentences. To revive enervated sentences, negate with verbs instead of with *not*. People often miss *not* when reading and thus misunderstand your sentence. This trick shortens your sentences and expresses your points vividly.

> *Before*: People often do not see *not* when reading and thus do not understand your sentence.

> *After*: People often miss *not* when reading and thus misunderstand your sentence.

Some of psychology's common phrases are aggressively, proudly passive. In any journal, you'll find psychologists "ivving it up": Their results are indicat*ive* of significance, the theory is reflect*ive* of its historical context, the data are support*ive* of the hypothesis. This is passive writing at its most flamboyant and unapologetic: The writer chose an awkward, passive form instead of a common, active form. Why not say the results indicate, the theory reflects, the data support? Delete all *to be* _____*ive of* phrases by rewriting the verb:

- to be indicative of = to indicate
- to be reflective of = to reflect
- to be supportive of = to support
- to be implicative of = to imply

I have a memory of reading *is confirmative of*—a false memory, I hope.

Only vigilance will stop wordy phrases from slithering into your sentences. I recently read an article that claimed that attitudes are emotional in nature. If attitudes are emotional in nature, what are they like in captivity? Will they reproduce like captive pandas? Psychologists who write *in nature* probably saw the movie *Out of Africa* too many times during their formative years. Unless you plan to submit your article to *National Geographic*, avoid *in nature*. Adjectives describe the natures of things, so *in nature* is always implied in an adjective. After this rant, I needn't describe why *in a _____ manner* is bad. Use adverbs— "people responded *rapidly*" instead of "people responded *in a rapid manner*"—to avoid a tragedy of manners.

Even active sentences can be limp and lifeless. Psychologists often start a sentence with "Research shows that . . . ," "Recent studies indicate that . . . ," "Many new findings suggest that . . . ," or "A monstrous amount of research conclusively proves that . . . ." These phrases add little to your meaning, and citations at the end of the sentence will show that research bolsters your point. You'll need these phrases occasionally—I use them in this book to contrast empirical facts with personal opinions—but avoid them when possible.

Writers hobble strong sentences by starting with lumpy phrases like "However . . . ," "For instance . . . ," and "For example . . . ." Move *however* into the first joint of the sentence:

> *Before*: However, recent findings challenge dual-process theories of persuasion.
>
> *After*: Recent findings, however, challenge dual-process theories of persuasion.

Relocate *for example* and *for instance* as well, but (in informal writing) keep *but* and *yet* at the start of the sentence. As an aside, remember that a poorly punctuated *however* can turn a compound sentence into a glorious run-on.

> *Before*: High self-efficacy enhances motivation for challenging tasks, however it reduces motivation if people perceive the task as easy.
>
> *After*: High self-efficacy enhances motivation for challenging tasks; however, it reduces motivation if people perceive the task as easy.

Write actively, but don't feel overwrought when you write passive sentences. Like all scientific writing, psychological writing involves impersonal agents such as concepts, theories, constructs, and relationships. We often have weak agents, such as *past research*, *cognitive dissonance theory*, or *the cognitive approach to anxiety disorders.* When readers can't easily form a mental image of the subject and its action—a theory making predictions, a concept correlating with another concept, a tradition influencing modern research—active sentences lose their punch. One solution to weak subjects—one favored by writers on a misguided quest to avoid anthropomorphism—is to replace impersonal agents like *cognitive dissonance theory* with *researchers*, as in *researchers studying cognitive dissonance theory*. I doubt that this helps. Vague subjects like *researchers* and *people interested in* are equally abstract, impersonal, and hard to imagine. And this approach can be misleading: Sometimes we're writing about cognitive dissonance theory, not about people who study it.

WRITE FIRST, REVISE LATER

Generating text and revising text are distinct parts of writing—don't do both at once. The goal of text generation is to throw confused, wide-eyed words on a page; the goal of text revision is to scrub the words clean so that they sound nice and make sense. Some writers—invariably struggling writers—try to write a pristine first draft, one free of flaws and infelicities. The quest for the perfect first draft is misguided. Writing this way is just too stressful: These writers compose a sentence; worry about it for 5 minutes; delete it; write it again; change a few words; and then, exasperated, move on to the next sentence. Perfectionism is paralyzing. Furthermore, writing sentence by sentence makes your text sound disjointed. The paragraph, not the sentence, is the basic unit of writing.

Master the rules of style, but don't let those rules paralyze you when you sit down to write. Revising while you generate text is like drinking decaffeinated coffee in the early morning: noble idea, wrong time. Your first drafts should sound like they were hastily translated from Icelandic by a nonnative speaker. Writing is part creation and part criticism, part id and part superego: Let the id unleash a discursive screed, and then let the superego evaluate it for correctness and appropriateness. Rejoice in writing your gnarled and impenetrable drafts, just as you rejoice in later stamping out your fuzzy phrases and unwanted words.

CONCLUSIONS

This chapter sought to make you self-conscious about your writing. Many individuals display inaccurate self-assessments of their deficient writing skill levels—or to borrow Zinsser's (2001) simple sentence: "Few people realize how badly they write" (p. 19). Strong, clear writing will make your work stand out from the crowd of shoddy, obtuse, pretentious, and mediocre manuscripts and grant proposals. People respect good writing. Reviewers of grant proposals know that clear writing requires clear thinking; journal editors appreciate a clean description of a good idea. Read some of the books listed in the back of this book, practice the principles of good writing when you generate and revise text, and never write *individuals* or *such that* again.

6

Writing Journal Articles

Psychology journals are like the mean jocks and aloof rich girls in every 1980s high school movie—they reject all but the beautiful and persistent. Writing a journal article combines all the elements that deter motivation: The probability of success is low; the likelihood of criticism and rejection is high; and the outcome, even if successful, isn't always rewarding. Doing research is fun; writing about the research is not. Despite this, we must write journal articles because science communicates through its journals. Conferences are great for meeting old friends and seeing what fellow researchers are doing, but conference presentations are neither peer reviewed nor archived. Publication is the natural end point of the process of research.

The field's file cabinets are full of unborn articles. I know many researchers who have a shameful backlog of data; some have unpublished data from the 1980s that they "hope to publish someday." Sure they will. Because psychology venerates journal articles above other forms of publication, the field has good resources

"I wrote another five hundred words. Can I have another cookie?"

that help beginning writers learn how to publish journal articles (e.g., American Psychological Association [APA], 2001; Sternberg, 2000). Most of those resources, however, have failed to address the hard motivational problems involved in writing articles. This chapter gives a practical and personal look at writing journal articles. It provides tips for writing stronger articles and advice for writing in the face of inevitable criticism and failure. The advice in this chapter won't make you love writing articles, but it will help you write more of them with less dread.

PRACTICAL TIPS FOR WRITING AN EMPIRICAL ARTICLE

Writing a journal article is like writing a screenplay for a romantic comedy: You need to learn a formula.

As odd as it sounds, you should be grateful for APA style. Once you learn what goes where—and what never goes where—you'll find it easy to write journal articles. If you don't own the latest *Publication Manual of the American Psychological Association* (APA, 2001), you should buy it.

Outlining and Prewriting

On my list of maladaptive practices that make writing harder, Not Outlining is pretty high—just above Typing With Scratchy Wool Mittens, just below Training My Dog to Take Dictation. Outlining is writing, not a prelude to "real writing." Writers who complain about "writer's block" are writers who don't outline. After trying to write blindly, they feel frustrated and complain about how hard it is to generate words. No surprise—you can't write an article if you don't know what to write. People who write a lot outline a lot. "Clear thinking becomes clear writing," said Zinsser (2001, p. 9). Get your thoughts in order before you try to communicate them to the world of science.

Writing an outline lets you make early decisions about your paper. How long do you want your paper to be? How much attention do you want to give to past research? Should this paper be a short report or a full-length research article? Most of these decisions are between you and your research, but I encourage you to be concise. After many years of bloated articles crowding the journals, psychology is moving toward shorter articles. Some prestigious journals publish only short articles (e.g., *Psychological Science*), and many others have recently created short reports sections. Short is good. Think about how you feel when you read journal articles. Do you wish that they would end sooner, or do you wish that the authors would keep their momentum going for another 14 pages? Don't cram everything into one paper. You can write a lot of papers in your career, so you can work an omitted idea into another paper or develop it into a paper of its own.

An inner audience—an image of who will read your paper—will help you with your writing decisions. How thoroughly should you describe competing theories of visual attention? Should you explain a statistical method, or should you assume that most readers will understand it? Other professionals in your area—the professors and graduate students who share your research interests or wish to learn more about the topic—are the biggest part of your audience. Write for this audience. Smaller groups within your audience include undergraduate students, journalists, people working in related fields, and a few eclectic readers (e.g., bloggers and humorists). Many of your readers speak English as a second or third language; keep them in mind when you're tempted to choose trendy, vapid words. To refine your inner audience, make a rough list of the journals that you would want to publish your paper. Journals such as *Journal of Experimental Psychology: General* and *Psychological Science* have broad audiences; other journals, such as *Visual Cognition* and *Self and Identity*, attract audiences of specialists. When writing for specialists, you can assume that your readers know the field's theories, findings, and methods. And write your paper with a smooth, professional tone. Your goal is to sound like a normal person with something worthwhile to say—don't be too serious or too casual.

The Title and Abstract

Most readers who come across your article will see only the title and abstract, so make them good. A title must balance generality and specificity: Say what your article is about, but don't be so specific that your article sounds technical and tedious. If tempted to write a trendy, topical, or comical title, think about how it will sound in 10 years. Will future researchers get the joke? In the digital age, readers find your article with electronic databases that store and search titles and abstracts. Include all the search keywords in your abstract that you want to yield your article. For my research on self-awareness, for example, I use synonyms like *self-focus*, *self-focused attention*, and *self-consciousness* in the abstract. It seems that nearly everyone writes the title and abstract last, so follow the herd.

Introduction

Your introduction conveys the significance or triviality of your research. Of the parts of your article, the introduction is most likely to be read instead of skimmed or skipped. As a result, it's the section that writers fear most. Some people warn beginning writers that there's no formula for an introduction (e.g., Kendall, Silk, & Chu, 2000). Nonsense—of course there's a formula. Good writers use a good formula; you'll recognize it.

- Start your introduction with an overview of the article, which should be only one or two paragraphs. In this overview, describe the general problem, question, or theory that motivated the research. The goal of this section is to justify the article's existence, to interest the reader, and to provide a framework that will help the reader understand the rest of the article.

- After your overview, start with a heading that introduces the second part of your introduction. The heading might resemble your title. This second section is the body of the introduction: Here you describe relevant theories, review past research, and discuss in more detail the question that motivated your research. Use headings and subheadings as signposts. If there are two theories, for instance, create a subheading for each one. Keep the second section focused on the problem you described in the first section.

- After the second section, write a heading called *The Present Experiments* or *The Present Research*. Thus far, you have given an overview of your problem (section 1) and reviewed the necessary theories and findings (section 2). By now, the reader understands your question's context and significance. In this third section, describe your experiments and explain how they answer this question—it might take one to four paragraphs, depending on the level of detail. Conclude this section with the heading that begins your Method section (*Method* or *Study 1*).

This formula introduces the reader to your problem (section 1), reviews theories and research relevant to the problem (section 2), and clearly states how your research will solve the problem (section 3). It leads the reader down a clear path, and it keeps the writer from straying into irrelevant areas. You'll find exceptions to this formula—for short reports, a single section with no headings might suffice—but it will serve you well for most of your papers.

Your introduction should introduce the research, not exhaustively review everything anyone has ever said about your problem. Brief reports may have crisp 2- to 3-page introductions; mammoth manuscripts submitted to journals that indulge windy writers may have 12- to 20-page introductions. When writing normal research articles, keep your introduction under 10 manuscript pages.

Method

Method sections aren't glamorous, but they reveal how carefully you conducted your research (Reis, 2000). A good method section allows another researcher to replicate your study. Like introductions, method sections follow a formula. Your method section will have several subsections. The first, *Participants* or *Participants and Design*, describes the size and characteristics of the sample and, for experiments, the experimental design. If your study involved equipment—such as physiological equipment, unusual software, response pads, or voice-activated response switches—you'll need a subsection called *Apparatus*. A *Measures* subsection is helpful for research that involved sets of scales, tests, and assessment tools, such as neurocognitive tests, interest inventories, and self-report measures of attitudes or individual differences.

After these subsections, you have the *Procedure* subsection, the heart of your method section. In this section, describe what you did and said. Reviewers pay close attention to the procedure subsection, and you don't want to look like you're hiding something. Provide a lot of detail about your independent variables and dependent variables. Your rhetorical goal is to connect your procedures with the procedures used in published articles. If your experiment used a manipulation that has been used before, cite representative past experiments, even if the manipulation is well-known. If you invented the manipulation, cite research that used similar manipulations or research that implies that your manipulation is reasonable. If your independent variable involved classifying people into groups (e.g., low and high social anxiety), describe the basis for the classification (cutoff scores, norms, conventions) and cite past research that used the same classification basis. Connecting your procedures to past research allays concerns about the validity of your methods.

Reviewers want to know how you measured your dependent variables. If your dependent variables are well established, cite articles that developed or used the scales. For professional tests, cite the test manuals as well as recent articles that used the tests. If your dependent variables were ad hoc, such as self-report items that you wrote, list each item and cite a paper that used similar items. For self-report scales, list the scale values—for example, 7-point scales can be 1 to 7, 0 to 6, or −3 to +3—along with any labels that anchored the scale (e.g., 1 = *not at all*, 7 = *extremely*). If your dependent measures were physiological or behavioral, briefly describe past research that supports the construct validity of your measure.

Papers that report a series of studies can save space by reporting variations from the first experiment's methods. If all three experiments used the same apparatus, for instance, you needn't describe the apparatus three times. When describing the later experiments, just say that they used the same equipment.

Results

The *Results* section describes your analyses. Beginning writers feel compelled to report every possible analysis of their data, probably because thesis and dissertation committees want to see such analyses. Journal articles should be crisp: Report only the results that bear on your problem. Bad results sections are long lists of numbers and statistical tests; good results sections create a story (Salovey, 2000). First, start your results section with analyses that inform the integrity of your study. This section might report the internal consistency of self-report scales, estimates of interrater agreement, analyses of manipulation checks, or the method of data reduction and treatment.

Second, describe your analyses in a logical sequence. There's no one way to do this—it depends on your methods and hypotheses—but try to cast your central findings into bold relief. Salovey (2000) suggested reporting your most interesting and important findings first. When describing results, don't mindlessly report test after test. For each test, remind the reader of your hypothesis, report the statistics, and then discuss what the tests mean. "But discussions of findings are for the general discussion!" protest beginning writers. This is a misunderstanding of what people learned in their undergraduate research methods classes. The results section isn't an exclusive club for numbers only. Don't just report a one-way analysis of variance and say it was significant. Describe your prediction, report the test, and describe what the findings mean. Which group was higher than the other? Was the pattern consistent with your prediction?

Third, use tables and figures to reduce the clutter of numbers that afflicts most results sections. My most common comment as a manuscript reviewer is, "The authors should present the descriptive statistics in a table." For experimental designs, make a table that presents the means, standard deviations, and cell sizes. To go the extra mile, include 95% confidence intervals—reviewers will appreciate your openness, and readers will be able to compute their own analyses of your data. For correlational designs, make a table that presents the means, standard deviations, sample sizes, confidence intervals, estimates of internal consistency, and a correlation matrix. With that information, a reader can create and test structural equation models of your data (Kline, 2005). There's no law against presenting data in both a figure and a table: The figure is for readers who want to see the pattern of data, and the table is for readers who want the dirty details.

Discussion

If your paper has several studies, a *Discussion* section follows each results section. These sections are narrower than the general discussion. They summarize the study's findings and discuss how the study informs the paper's central problem. Discussions should also address limitations in the experiment, such as unexpected results or problems with the procedure. Consider creating a *Results and Discussion* section if your discussion section merely summarizes the results.

General Discussion

The *General Discussion* steps back and looks at your findings in light of other theories and past research.

Start your general discussion with a brief overview of your problem and your findings: One or two paragraphs will usually be enough. Good general discussions have little in common—your problem, methods, and research area will dictate what you ought to discuss—except that they are usually short. Think about how you read general discussions. Do you skim them, skip them, or complain about the author's fruitless discussion of every minor aspect of the research? Try to keep the general discussion shorter than the introduction. If you like, conclude the general discussion with a one paragraph summary of the entire article.

Your undergraduate research-methods teacher told you to end your general discussion with a section on limitations; your thesis committee probably wanted this section, too. Describing limitations is a useful educational exercise, but it's often pointless in an article intended for a professional journal. Some limitations are generic to all research. Yes, it would have been nice to have a larger and more representative sample; yes, it would have been nice to have included even more measures; yes, it's conceivable that a future study that uses different measures with a larger sample will find a different pattern of results. Don't insult your audience—everyone knows that these limitations inhere in all research. Other limitations are generic to an area of research. Cognitive psychologists know that they use contrived computer-based tasks; social psychologists know that they use convenience samples of undergraduates. Specialists know that your research shares the area's generic limitations. Don't waste time stating the obvious. Instead, devote space to limitations specific to your research. But don't merely raise your study's limitations—raise them and then make a good case for why they aren't as grim as they look.

References

Your *References* section documents the sources that influenced the ideas in your paper. By embedding your work within the field of science, your references say a lot about how you view your research. Be selective— you needn't cite everything you read on the topic, and you should never cite books or articles that you haven't read. Scholars who have read those articles can tell that you cribbed the reference from another source. Although not as glamorous as an introduction or as brawny as a results section, a reference section deserves to be done well. As a reviewer, I see a lot of sloppy reference sections. Lazy writers often commit grievous crimes against APA style and fail to include references for articles cited in the text. "What's the big deal?" some would say; "They're just references." Your friends down the hall can see your sloppy reference list; the critical, anonymous peer reviewers should see your best work.

Seasoned writers use their references to increase the odds of getting desired reviewers. When editors consider possible reviewers for your paper, they often flip to the references to see whom you cited. I'm not sure if this trick works, but it probably can't hurt. Also, cite your past work in your new manuscripts. Self-citations strike some writers as shameless self-aggrandizement. I've met writers, invariably beginners, who were reluctant to cite themselves. Citing your past work connects your latest article with your stream of work. If someone is interested enough in your work to read your latest article, he or she would probably be interested in reading your other articles, too. Self-citations make it easy for readers to learn about them.

SUBMITTING YOUR MANUSCRIPT

Your manuscript is ready to be submitted to a journal when it's clear, well-written, and as perfect as possible. If you think "I'll just send it now and clean it up later when I resubmit it," stop thinking and start revising. Only masochists submit rough drafts to journals. Pristine manuscripts grab the attention and respect of reviewers and show the editor that you're a serious professional who can be counted on to do revisions quickly and thoroughly. Before submitting your pristine manuscript, read the instructions to authors posted on the journal's Web site. Read these directions closely, because journals have different submission guidelines. Most journals accept electronic submissions, either by e-mail or through a Web-based submission portal.

Regardless of how you submit your manuscript, you'll need to write a cover letter to the editor. Some people write a simple, standard letter; others write an extended exegesis on the merits and importance of the manuscript. I asked some friends who have edited major journals about their preferences. They unanimously preferred a simple letter with the essential boilerplate: the name of the manuscript, the author's mailing and electronic addresses, and the standard assurances that the manuscript isn't under review elsewhere and that the data were collected according to the field's ethical standards. One person, an associate editor, noted that he often didn't read the author's cover letter because the submission portal made it hard to retrieve. Another told me that she wanted to be persuaded by the manuscript, not by a letter about the manuscript.

In your cover letter, you can suggest possible reviewers and request that certain people not serve as reviewers. I've heard from editor friends that they're more likely to honor the "do not review" list than the friends and cronies list. Perhaps one of the associate editors at the journal would be perfect for reviewing your manuscript. If you like, you can ask the editor to assign the manuscript to that associate editor. (Although I've made this request several times, my manuscript was never assigned to that person.)

Understanding Reviews and Resubmitting Your Manuscript

While idly leafing through old issues of *Child Development*, I read an editorial from the early 1970s. The editor described the peer review process and mentioned that the average response time was 6 weeks. Think about this. Thirty years ago, an author mailed a stack of hard copies to an editor, who in turn mailed the copies to reviewers. After composing their comments on typewriters, the reviewers stamped and mailed their reviews. The editor typed an action letter, saving a carbon copy for the files, and then mailed the letter and reviews to the author. Today's authors, editors, and reviewers correspond electronically, often through sophisticated Web-based portals that manage the submission, send reminders to reviewers and editors, and eliminate all delays due to postal mail. Thank technology while waiting for your reviews.

When the editor's action letter arrives, he or she will usually summarize the key points made by the reviewers and state a decision about the manuscript. The decision can take three forms: The manuscript has been accepted, the door is open for a resubmission, or the door is closed.

- Acceptance decisions are easy to interpret. The editor says the manuscript has been accepted and tells you to complete some forms; sometimes the editor accepts a manuscript pending minor changes. It's rare that the first submission of a manuscript is accepted. Even when they like the manuscript, editors usually want authors to shorten it or add information. Some editors occasionally accept manuscripts with no changes required—one more reason to submit strong first drafts.

- When the door is open, the editor is willing to consider a revised version of your manuscript. This category ranges from encouraging letters that imply likely acceptance to discouraging letters that imply a long slog of revision. Wide-open doors involve easy changes, such as rewriting parts of the text or adding information. Barely open doors involve effortful changes, such as collecting more data and rethinking the conceptual basis for your research. Sometimes, editors say that they'll treat heavily revised manuscripts as new submissions.

- When the door is closed, the editor never wants to see your manuscript again. Sometimes, closed-door rejections encourage you to submit your manuscript elsewhere; other times, the editor mails you a personal shredder for destroying all known copies of the manuscript. If the door is closed, don't antagonize the editor by resubmitting the manuscript.

Even seasoned researchers are often uncertain if an editor is willing to consider a revised version of a manuscript. The word *reject* doesn't necessarily mean that you can't resubmit the manuscript. Many editors use *reject* to refer to any manuscript that they aren't accepting. They can reject your first draft but intend to accept a revised draft. I suspect that some conflict-averse editors use discouraging open-door letters to brush off authors—"We're happy to consider a revised manuscript that includes three new experiments and a rewritten Introduction and General Discussion." When uncertain, show your reviews to a friend or write a brief e-mail to the editor to ask for a clarification.

If the door is open for resubmission, consider whether you're willing to do the work. An editor might want new data, new analyses, and extensive rewriting. Is the project worth the effort? Your default decision should be to do the work necessary for resubmission. Remember that all journals have high rejection rates. By receiving an invitation to resubmit the manuscript, you have cheated the gods of rejection rates. If the journal is prestigious, you should do the effortful changes, such as adding another experiment. If the manuscript is low in priority, you might want to send it elsewhere instead of devoting more time to data collection.

After you commit to revise and resubmit your manuscript, you need to make a plan for your revision. Examine the editor's letter and the reviews and extract the action points. (Don't say *actionable* points—it's a slippery slope to abominations like *drinkable* and *do-able*.) Action points are targets for change. Read the editor's letter and the reviews, and underline each comment that implies a change. It might be a change in the text—adding something, deleting something, rewording something—or a change in the analyses. It might be a major change like adding or deleting an experiment. Many reviews are discursive and meandering; a long review might have only a few action points. After you identify the action points, revise the manuscript quickly. In chapter 3, I argued that revisions should be high-priority project goals. They're close to publication, so don't slow down now. Some editors give deadlines for submitting a revision, such as 60 days or 90 days.

When you resubmit your manuscript, you'll need to send a cover letter that describes how you handled the criticisms and comments. Should you write a brief letter that highlights the major changes, or should you write a comprehensive list of all the changes? My informal survey of journal editors found unanimous support for lengthy, detailed resubmission letters. Most of the editors complained about authors who wrote skimpy letters ("We changed a lot; we hope you like it"), authors who resisted making any changes, and authors who discussed things they changed but didn't discuss why they ignored some of the reviewers' comments. By showing precisely what you did and didn't change, a detailed letter makes it easier for an editor to accept your revised manuscript.

Your resubmission letter must be detailed and constructive; you must address each action point openly and thoroughly. People who publish a lot write great resubmission letters. These letters sell your changes and show the editor that you're a serious scientist who takes feedback well. Brief, vague letters make authors look as if they have something to hide; long, detailed letters make the authors look constructive and sincere. Be polite and professional—your letter is not the place to belittle a lazy reviewer, to defend your honor from a belligerent reviewer, or to flaunt your superior skills in statistics. It's tempting, but take the scientific high ground instead.

I collected a stash of strong resubmission letters written by colleagues who have published a lot or who have edited journals. Here's what you should do.

- Begin your resubmission letter by thanking the editor for his or her comments and for the opportunity to submit a revised draft. Even though you would have preferred flat-out acceptance, you still managed to beat the journal's rejection rate.
- Create headings for each set of action points. Many writers organize their letters according to who gave the comments. A typical structure is to create a *Your Comments* heading followed by *Reviewer 1's Comments*, *Reviewer 2's Comments*, and so forth. Within each heading, exhaustively address each point made by that reviewer using numbered lists. Numbered lists simplify the letter and make it easy to refer to points made earlier. For example, perhaps both reviewers suggested adding more detail about your sample. Although you discussed this under *Reviewer 1's Comments*, discuss it under *Reviewer 2's Comments*, too. Simply dispatch it by noting the comment and referring to the number of your earlier discussion.

- Tackle each action point with a three-part system. First, summarize the comment or criticism. Second, describe what you did in response to this comment; cite specific page numbers in your manuscript whenever possible. Third, discuss how this resolves the comment.

- The editor doesn't expect you to follow each suggestion, but he or she expects you to discuss why you didn't follow it. I have seen resubmission letters in which the authors stubbornly refused to make trivial changes such as combining small tables into a bigger table or chopping 10% off the manuscript. Pick your battles. If you don't follow a comment, give that comment extra detail in your cover letter. Justify why you didn't make the change.

- Be professional; don't be fawning and obsequious. The editor doesn't think the reviewers are geniuses, and he or she doesn't expect you to refer to the reviewers' comments as masterful, great, brilliant, or insightful. Put yourself in the editor's role. Would an ingratiating cover letter persuade you, or would you think, "This person is a dork"?

Good resubmission letters will make you look like a serious scholar—because you are. People who deal constructively with criticism deserve to be published. Sometimes it takes me longer to write a resubmission letter than to revise the manuscript. The resubmission letter for one of my manuscripts (Silvia & Gendolla,

2001) was 3,200 words, about the length of chapter 5 of this book. Some of my published articles have fewer than 3,200 words.

"But What if They Reject My Paper?"

Many writers fear receiving negative feedback, getting rejected, or being wrong. A classic theory of achievement motivation proposed two motives that affect performance: a need to achieve success and a need to avoid failure (Atkinson, 1964). Situational factors can amplify these motives, and writing journal articles seems to evoke a writer's need to avoid failure. Many writers—particularly people new to the world of academic writing—ruminate about rejection. They worry about what the editor will say; they imagine a reviewer scowling while reading their manuscript; they dread the rejection letter in their in-box.

People's need to avoid failure makes them ask questions like "But what if they reject my paper?" Of course they'll reject your paper. You should write your paper on the assumption that the journal will reject it. Theories of decision making point out that base rates are the most rational estimates for decisions made under uncertainty. If a journal rejects 80% of submissions, then the base rate of acceptance is 20%. In the absence of any other information, the rational estimate is that your paper has a 20% chance of acceptance. Because no journals have rejection rates below 50%, I assume that each paper I submit will be rejected. It's the only rational conclusion, and my faith in rationality is supported by the amount of rejections I receive.

"That's bleak," you might say. "How can you be motivated to write if you expect rejection?" First, people shouldn't be motivated to write—they should simply stick to a writing schedule, mental rain or mental shine. Second, beginning writers seem to think that they're the only people who get rejected. Researchers who publish a lot of articles receive a lot of rejections. Psychology's most prolific writers get more rejections per year than other writers get in a decade. I find the base rates of rejection oddly comforting. I feel less uncertain about what will happen, I don't feel so bad when my paper is rejected, and I prevent myself from indulging in fruitless fantasies of imagining my work in print before I finish the manuscript.

You'll write better when you expect rejection, because you'll mute the need to avoid failure. Writers motivated by failure avoidance write papers that sound defensive, wishy-washy, and uncertain. Instead of trying to look good, they try not to look bad. Readers can feel the fear. Writers motivated by the need to achieve success, in contrast, write papers that sound confident and controlled. These writers focus on the strengths of the work, assert the importance of the research, and convey a persuasive sense of confidence.

And as for whether reviewers will hate your paper: Yes, sometimes they will hate your paper. Here's an excerpt from a blistering rejection that I received recently. In summarizing the reviews, the editor wrote,

Both reviewers believed your manuscript was below publication standards. One reviewer believes that the manuscript did not make a significant contribution, misinterpreted opposing theories, offered conclusions not well tied to research evidence, and was plagued by imprecise writing. The other reviewer believes that the manuscript falls short of advancing a complete and accurate model, makes unsupported claims, omits general important studies and ideas, and makes some faulty theoretical assumptions and criticisms.

And that was the editor's cordial summary of the reviews—one of the reviewers was mean. But that's okay. I extracted action points from the reviews, revised the manuscript, and submitted it to a different journal. Given base rates, it'll probably get rejected again.

Sometimes, rejections are unfair, mean, and poorly reasoned. Sometimes you can tell that the editor or reviewers didn't read your paper carefully. Resist the urge to complain to the editor. I have heard of people writing the editor an angry letter that denounced the reviewers as lazy incompetents. Those letters never work, probably because the editor is often friends with one or more of the reviewers. Some people recommend writing this embittered letter but not mailing it. That's even more irrational—why waste your scheduled writing time with fruitless venting? Spend your time revising your paper instead. The world is unfair ($p < .001$), so take what you can from the reviews, revise your paper, and send it somewhere else.

To write a lot, you should rethink your mental models of rejection and publication. Rejections are like a sales tax on publications: The more papers you publish, the more rejections you receive. Following the tips in this book will make you the most rejected writer in your department.

"But What if They Make Me Change Everything?"

Journals are science's public record. Your article will be printed on acid-free paper and archived on library shelves for eternity, however long that will be. Scientific progress is faster when people connect their work to others' work, identify problems in their own research, analyze data properly, and avoid misleading descriptions of what they or others have accomplished. Journals are not a forum for psychologists to rant about their personal opinions—that's what newsletters and conferences are for. Science holds published research to high standards and uses peer review to provide quality control. You will be asked to change your paper; sometimes those changes will be extensive. If this bothers you, then you'll hate to hear that published articles are always better than the first drafts. Published research is more focused, less confrontational, and more circumspect. Peer review is irksome for authors, but it's central to psychology's scientific mission.

Coauthoring Journal Articles

It might take a village to conduct a research project, but the villagers should keep their mitts off the article.

I asked a lot of people how they wrote papers that had several authors, and nearly everyone said that one author did most of the writing. The authors collectively develop and approve an outline, but one person generates the text. When the paper is done, all of the authors read it, provide comments, or rewrite parts as needed. A variation of this involves assigning sections to different authors. A common division of labor assigns one person to write the method and results sections and another person to write everything else. I did find, however, some people who literally wrote together. One pair of writers pulled two chairs in front of a computer, talked about what to say, and passed the keyboard back and forth. Another person said that he and a colleague wrote grants by putting two computers in a room and writing together. This system allowed them to work out kinks in the proposal and to interrupt each other with questions. Maybe a few villagers should touch the article, after all.

Be careful whom you write with. Don't commit to research collaborations without discussing who will write the manuscript. If your collaborator is a binge writer, be skeptical of assurances about writing the paper quickly or expressions of excitement about the research. Enthusiasm isn't commitment. If you can't trust your coauthor, write the first draft yourself as the first author. Sometimes, after you've done the hard work of writing, your coauthor takes forever to provide comments on the manuscript. Set deadlines for your coauthors when you give them the first draft. Say, "I want to submit this within 2 weeks, so get comments to me before then." Submit the paper when the deadline passes. A friend of mine sent a derelict coauthor an e-mail with "You're off the paper" as the subject. That worked.

Derelict coauthors are a big problem for graduate students, particularly when the coauthor is the faculty advisor. Many students complain that their advisors are holding up their articles—some advisors take months or years to comment on manuscripts that the student wrote. It's hard for graduate students to push their advisors around, so sneakier strategies are in order. Try to get someone else to push your advisor around. Why not complain to another faculty member, the department chair, or the director of graduate studies? If that doesn't work, photocopy this section from this book and anonymously leave it in your advisor's mailbox. The brash can attach it to a copy of their manuscript. Finally, set a deadline for your advisor and submit the paper yourself. The unwillingness to read a student's paper and provide comments shows a lack of commitment to graduate training and the process of science. Say, "I really need to submit this within 4 weeks," and remind the person 2 weeks and 3 weeks later.

Writing Review Articles

After writing a few empirical articles, it might be time to think about review articles. A lot of people read review articles: researchers looking for new ideas, students learning a new area, teachers preparing lectures, and policymakers checking out what psychology has to say. Empirical articles are easy to write once you master the formula provided by APA style, but review articles are tricky. The motivational issues are the same—stick to your writing schedule—but the organizational issues are different. Researchers can write many kinds of reviews, with different goals, structures, and methods (Cooper, 2003), and there's no formula.

Because review articles are so diverse, you'll need to do a lot of planning. Your first decision concerns the scope of your article. Some review journals, such as *Current Directions in Psychological Science*, publish crisp, short reviews. Other journals, such as *Psychological Review*, *Psychological Bulletin*, and *Review of General Psychology*, publish long, comprehensive articles. How long will your article be? Your second decision concerns the audience for your article. In addition to its general review journals, psychology has many review journals devoted to special topics, such as *Clinical Psychology Review* and *Personality and Social Psychology Review*. Do you want to reach a broad swath of your field, or are you writing for an audience of specialists?

After you have a sense of your article's scope and audience, you'll need an outline that develops its central idea. Review articles must make an original point; they shouldn't merely review what has been done. The worst review articles string together descriptions of other articles. Reading an endless litany of study after study—one article found this, and another experiment found this, and another study found this—is like watching laundry spinning in a dryer, except that something good eventually comes out of a dryer. To develop your original point, think about the distinction that creativity researchers make between *problem solving* and *problem finding* (Sawyer, 2006). A problem-solving review describes a problem (such as a controversial or ambiguous area of research) and proposes a solution to the problem (such as a new theory, model, or interpretation). A problem-finding review develops new concepts and identifies topics that deserve more attention. Good review articles involve both problem solving and problem finding. Resolving a conflict between two theories, for example, usually implies new directions for future research. What's the problem that you want to solve? What new ideas come from your solution?

A review article's most common flaw is the absence of an original point. Some authors rehash research without drawing a conclusion; other authors describe competing theories without offering a resolution. This flaw has two causes. First, writers can't develop a new idea if they don't have any new ideas. It happens. After reading a massive body of work, you might learn that you have nothing original to add. If so, don't stubbornly write a review article to justify the time spent reading the articles. Second, some writers don't outline. They sit down with a stack of articles, grimly describe each study, and then tack a short "critical summary" to the end of the paper. A complex project requires a strong outline—without one, your original point will be eclipsed by the mass of past research. Instead of writing review articles, people who don't outline should drive to the local animal shelter and adopt a dog, one that will love them despite their self-defeating and irrational habits.

If you have an original point, don't hide it under a bushel—or under a laundry basket, if you don't own any bushels. Your original point should appear within the first few paragraphs of your article. The first part of your review article should introduce the article's central ideas, outline the article, and prefigure the original point that you plan to make. It's tempting to write a chronological review—first Theory 1, then Theory 2, and then a critical analysis—but don't do it. Reviews contain a lot of information, so your readers need a good outline at the start of the article. Unlike good mystery novels, good review articles reveal the culprit on the first page.

Review articles sound hard to write, and they are. That's why binge writers rarely write review articles: There's so much to read, so much to digest, and so much to write. But reflective, disciplined writers have nothing to fear. If you have a schedule, it doesn't matter that review articles are hard work: You have clear goals, an inviolable schedule, and good habits, so it's just a matter of time before you finish your review article. After you decide to write one, spend some of your scheduled writing time getting advice.

Baumeister and Leary (1997) wrote an excellent guide to writing narrative reviews; you'll also find good advice in articles by Bem (1995), Cooper (2003), and Eisenberg (2000).

CONCLUSIONS

When struggling to write their first article, some writers lament, "Why would they care about my research?" If *they* refers to the world at large, I can assure you that they are uninterested in your research. But if *they* refers to researchers in your area, then you should expect some interest in your article. Remember that you're writing a technical article for an audience of specialists that shares your interests. Your paper might be rejected once or twice before it finds a good home, but a good paper will always find a home. To write good articles, master the article formula, submit pristine first drafts, and craft excellent resubmission letters. You'll find that the world of journals isn't scary: It's merely slow.

7

Writing Books

The great psychologists are remembered for their great books. No one reads the journal articles that Gordon Allport and Clark Hull wrote; people read *Pattern and Growth in Personality* (Allport, 1961) and *Principles of Behavior* (Hull, 1943) instead. This chapter is about writing books. If you would like to write a book, you won't find much practical advice about how to do it. Psychology's obsession with journal articles has inspired a lot of books, chapters, and articles about how to publish articles (e.g., Sternberg, 2000); there are few resources for aspiring book writers. As a result, this chapter is more personal than the others. It shares tips I learned the hard way while writing my books (Duval & Silvia, 2001; Silvia, 2006) and passes along good advice I received from generous book veterans.

You may be tempted to skip this chapter. "I'll *never* write a book. Writing a meager article is hard enough for me," you might think. Maybe. Writing a book is like writing anything else: You sit down and type. Books take longer than articles, but that's merely a matter of sticking to your writing schedule. While writing a grant proposal, T. Shelley Duval (who co-authored the classic book *A Theory of Objective Self-Awareness*; Duval & Wicklund, 1972) said, "I could write another book in the time it's taking to write this grant." (He was right—I spent fewer days writing this book's first draft than I spent writing a recent funded grant.) Writing a book is more intellectually rewarding than writing an article. Books matter more than journal articles, chapters in edited books, and edited books, and they offer a chance to tackle big questions and to draw controversial conclusions.

WHY WRITE A BOOK?

Meeting writers of good books motivated me to try writing a book—I thought it might be fun. As an undergraduate I worked with T. Shelley Duval. I remember that I found it weird to read his book and then talk about it with him. Many of the social psychologists I met during graduate school at the University of Kansas had written great books (e.g., Batson, Schoenrade, & Ventis, 1993; Brehm, 1966). Larry Wrightsman alone had written around two dozen (e.g., Wrightsman, 1999; Wrightsman & Fulero, 2004), and the late Fritz Heider's (1958) legendary book *The Psychology of Interpersonal Relations* still backlit the department.

People write scholarly books for different reasons. Many authors told me that they were curious to learn what they thought about a topic. Writing to learn is a good way to develop a sophisticated understanding of a complex problem (Zinsser, 1988). After writing your book, you'll have a decade's worth of research ideas. Others told me that a scholarly book was the capstone for a series of journal articles. When people wanted to wrap up a line of research, they wrote a book that summarized what they did and that motivated other researchers to tackle the remaining problems. For some writers, books are the only way to convey the complexity of their research. Researchers in the history of psychology, for example, write a lot of books because they have book-length problems. Some people simply think that it would be fun to write a book.

Perhaps you want to write a textbook. Teaching is central to psychology's scientific mission—a good textbook translates the knotty language of journal articles into the vernacular of daily life. Psychology always needs good textbooks. Many writers are attracted to textbook writing by the allure of royalties. A few textbooks make their authors rich, but most don't. Many textbooks fall flat and fail: The book is published, few instructors adopt it, and the publisher declines to print a second edition. Even the best textbooks—books that are integrative, ambitious, and forward looking—often meet this ignominious end. Because they don't see or hear about these books, people underestimate the number of textbooks that never stick. If a book doesn't go to a second edition, it goes out of print and is thus out of the market. If you're extrinsically motivated by money, find other reasons to write your textbook, such as a burning interest in sitting in a chair and typing.

How to Write Your Book in Two Easy Steps and One Hard Step

Step 1: Find a Coauthor

Writing a book is like repainting a bathroom—it's more fun when you have a partner. For your first book, consider finding a coauthor. You probably have some good friends who share your research interests. Why not ask them if they want to jump aboard? Coauthors are nice for some obvious reasons. Two authors can write a book faster than one author; this frees your writing time for other projects, such as manuscripts and grant proposals. Furthermore, a coauthor with different scholarly interests can complement your expertise, leading to a richer book. And coauthors are nice for some subtle reasons. Book authors face hard decisions about structure, organization, and coherence. If you're the only author, no one can help you with these hard choices. Your coauthor will be the only other person who understands the context of these decisions. If you can't find a coauthor or if your book is best written alone, consider finding a mentor. Do you have a friend or colleague who can advise you about the vagaries of book writing?

Pick a coauthor who writes a lot. This is obvious advice, but disasters happen when a productive writer and an unproductive writer decide to write a book together. Don't confuse enthusiasm with commitment. Has your potential coauthor written a book before? Has your coauthor published journal articles? Do you think that your coauthor is a productive writer? Don't get your book or your friendship into trouble. The productive writer complains, "What's wrong with him? Why won't he just sit down and write?" The unproductive writer complains, "What's her problem? She should get off my back and stop hounding me." A productive writer and an unproductive writer can still write a book together if both writers understand the division of labor. The productive writer can generate the text and the unproductive writer can develop outlines, provide critical comments on drafts of chapters, and revise parts of the book. If the unproductive coauthor has special expertise, he or she would make a good nonwriting coauthor.

Step 2: Plan Your Book

Some writers are oddly stubborn about outlining, even writers who know better. Be forewarned: It's impossible to write a book without a plan. Books are too big. The first step in writing a book—a step that could take months—is developing a strong table of contents. Develop your table of contents by brainstorming about what you think your book is about. As you brainstorm, you'll see a hierarchical structure to your ideas—the higher order ideas will be your chapters. Some authors write many brief chapters; others write fewer long chapters. As a rough guide, a typical scholarly book has between 8 and 14 chapters, and a typical textbook has between 12 and 20 chapters.

Your table of contents can evolve as you write. As you become immersed in your book, you'll develop new ideas and rethink your old ones. You might add a new chapter, combine two shorter than expected chapters, or cleave a long chapter in two. That's fine, but don't start writing without a sturdy table of contents. I probably spent 2 months mulling over this book's table of contents before I began writing the chapters.

Nested within the table of contents is an outline for each chapter. You should be able to describe, within a few paragraphs, what each chapter is about. You need chapter outlines for two reasons. First, writing a book is hard, and only fools and dilettantes try to write a book when ignorant of what will go into each chapter. You needn't extensively outline each chapter or even know everything you want to say, but you must have a firm sense of each chapter's purpose and how it contributes to the book's overall purpose. Second, to get a book contract, you'll need to describe each chapter to prospective publishers. Reviewers of your book proposal will scrutinize your table of contents to see how carefully you've thought about your book.

Just as your painting partner can help clean the brushes, your writing partner can help with the outlining. In the outlining stage—the first stage involving real writing—you and your coauthor will probably disagree about what to write about. This is fine—these disagreements illustrate the trade-off inherent in writing with a coauthor. When writing alone, you don't have to strike compromises, but on the hard days, you'll have to face a monster of your own making. When writing with a coauthor, you'll disagree about the book's content, organization, and emphasis. Compromise might bother you, but a good coauthor drags your mental cart out of its deep ruts. Two brains are much better than one.

Step 3: Write the Damn Thing

By now, even the dimmest reader has discerned this book's simple message: To write a lot, you must make a schedule and stick to it. That's how you write a book. Don't wait for the summer, and don't wait for a sabbatical. Even unapologetic binge writers can write a few chapters of a book during a sabbatical, but 12 months is rarely enough time to write all the chapters. Books get shipwrecked when binge authors resume their normal duties of teaching, research, and service. Being a bit dim myself, I learned this simple message the hard way. I started writing *Exploring the Psychology of Interest* (2006) during a postdoctoral year at the University of Hamburg. With a quiet office, strong German coffee, and few obligations, I unleashed much of the book within 6 months of binge writing. Because I didn't write according to a schedule, the book derailed when I started a tenure-track job.

It's tempting to skip from chapter to chapter, working on the fun parts and ignoring the hard parts. An author using this method could write several hundred pages without completing a chapter. It's deflating to run out of easy parts, so tackle the chapters in order. Several authors suggested starting with chapter 2, working in order, and writing the first chapter and the preface last. This is good advice because books can wriggle away from their authors. Many authors say that they never ended up with the book they intended to write: The final book is better, they say, but unexpectedly different. You can't introduce a book that you haven't read, so wait to see what you wrote before saying what you'll write.

Writing a book involves monstrous amounts of reading, research, and filing. One of the best tips I ever got was to organize my resources by chapter, not by topic. Authors quickly think of their books in terms of chapters—"that article would fit well in chapter 4," they say. "I'll use that quote to end chapter 8." If your mental schema for your book is organized according to chapters, you should organize your resources by chapter as well. Authors of books that went to several editions said that this system made it easy to organize resources for the next edition.

As with articles, you should monitor your progress on your book. It's easy to lose sight of long-range writing projects. While writing a book, I keep a chart that tracks how much I've written. Table 7.1 displays the chart for my interest book (Silvia, 2006). The

TABLE 7.1 Writing Chart

Chapter	Pages	Words	First draft	Revised draft	Chapter title
1	10	2,770	Done	Done	Introduction
2	23	5,830	Done	Done	Interest as an Emotion
3	41	10,952	Done	Done	What Is Interesting?
4	24	6,596	Done	Done	Interest and Learning
5	32	8,583	Done	Done	Interest, Personality, and Individual Differences
6	23	6,301	Done	Done	Interests and Motivational Development
7	29	7,838	Done	Done	How Do Interests Develop? Bridging Emotion and Personality
8	33	8,892	Done	Done	Interests and Vocations
9	21	5,609	Done	Done	Comparing Models of Interest
10	11	3,003	Done	Done	Conclusion: Looking Back, Looking Ahead
References	63	14,269	Done	Done	References
TOTAL	310	80,643			

Note. The writing chart that I used to monitor my book about interest (Silvia, 2006).

chart has columns for the chapter number and title. For each chapter, I monitored the number of pages and words. (Most writers measure a manuscript's length in pages, but most editors and publishers measure length in words.) Formulas embedded in the chart automatically calculated the total numbers of pages and words. The chart also marked whether the first and revised drafts were finished. You can add more rows and columns for your book. If your book has two authors, for example, you can create a column that records who is supposed to write each chapter. If the chapters have deadlines, as textbook chapters often do, then you can list them in a column.

How to Find a Publisher

When you read some of the books listed in "Good Books About Writing" at the back of this book, you'll notice that many of the authors described their struggles finding agents and publishers. In *The Writer's Book of Hope*, for example, Ralph Keyes (2003) told incredible stories of best sellers that had been rejected by dozens of publishers. Fortunately for psychologists, academic publishing is nothing like the world of trade publishing. In the real world—that place you lived before you went to grad school—there are thousands of authors vying for the attention of publishers, and each book is financially risky for the publishers. In the academic world, few people write books. Because of the small pool of possible authors, academic publishers want to cultivate strong relationships with people who write books. Scholarly publishing has fewer risks than trade publishing. Academic books have stable niche markets—university libraries, college courses—and time-tested ways of reaching their specialty audiences. Some academic publishers are not-for-profit organizations. If you're writing a good book, publishers want to talk with you about it.

After you have finished a couple of chapters, you need to make a first contact with book editors. The first contact approach favored by extraterrestrials—abducting people from their beds and tickling them with probes—is inappropriate for your first book. Instead, talk with editors at a conference. It's easy to pick out the book editors in the conference crowd: They're better dressed than the professors and graduate students, and they're standing next to big tables containing lots of books. "I thought they were there to sell books," you might say. Sure, selling and promoting books are two big reasons publishers set up tables at conferences. Book editors also go to conferences to cultivate contacts with potential authors and to check in on authors with books in progress. They want people to go up to them and talk about ideas for books. Just wander up to a publisher's table and ask if you can talk with someone about a book you're writing. You'll find their interest in your book refreshing because your colleagues in your agraphia group are probably sick of hearing about it.

The book writers I surveyed disagreed about how much an author should write before contacting a publisher. Some writers seek a contract early; others write the entire book before seeking a contract. Put some thought into this decision. Before you have a contract, you have made a deal only with yourself to write your book. It's bad to break a deal with yourself, but you won't lose money or anger anyone else—it's a matter between you and your sense of shame. But after you have a contract, your book exists officially and financially. If you break this deal, you'll appear unprofessional, your editor will be angry, and you'll owe the publisher money if you accepted an advance. Don't sign a contract until you know that your deal with yourself is unbreakable. Duval and I got a contract for our book before doing any writing; I sought a contract for my interest book after writing two chapters. For the venerable tome you're reading now, I wrote the entire first draft before contacting APA Books.

If intrigued by your book, editors will encourage you to send them a *book proposal*. You can find proposal guidelines on every publisher's Internet page. The typical proposal asks the author to describe the book's mission, intended audience, and major competitors. You'll need to provide a detailed table of contents, usually with several paragraphs that describe each chapter, and you should include sample chapters to show that you're serious. You may be asked to suggest people to review the proposal. The publishers will want to know a lot about you, too. Publishers know that writing a book is easier imagined than done. If you haven't written a book before, the editor may insist on seeing sample chapters.

Unlike journal articles, book proposals can be submitted simultaneously to several publishers. To save everyone's time, don't send a proposal to a publisher that you wouldn't want to publish your book. Many fine publishers with excellent reputations for dealing honorably with authors publish psychology books. When considering possible publishers, look for those with a strong presence in the area you're writing about. One publisher might have a book series devoted to the area. The publisher will send your proposal to peer reviewers, often to people whose books they have published. Sometimes the publisher sends you the reviewers' comments; sometimes they keep them. Either way, if your book sounds good, several publishers might offer you a contract.

A book contract is a big deal—it's not like the contract you sign at the video rental store, so read it carefully. Here are some standard parts of a book contract.

- The contract will specify a *delivery date*—that's when you let the book out of your grubby, coffee-stained mittens and give it to the publisher. Sometimes a publisher sets a series of delivery dates. Textbook publishers, for instance, often want a certain number of chapters by certain months. Put a lot of thought into the delivery date—2 years from the date of the contract is common. If you have been monitoring your writing, you know how many words you write per day and how often you write. Be empirical: Use your statistics to estimate a delivery date.

- Authors and publishers both care about royalties. It's common to have different rates for paperback and hardcover copies and to have the rates increase as more copies are sold. A contract often specifies exceptions to these rates, such as royalties authors earn on the rights to foreign translations. For many copies—remaindered books and complimentary copies, for instance—neither the author nor the publisher profits.

- Publishers entice authors with advances, and authors are irrationally enticed by them. Remember, this money is an advance on your royalties from the book—it isn't a signing bonus. If you don't need an advance you can decline it. If you'd rather have some of your royalties sooner rather than later, then discuss the advance with your editor. Advances are helpful if you plan to pay someone to proofread the page proofs or to make the book's figures.

- The contract will say who is responsible for handling permissions (requests to reprint material from other sources), for creating the book's figures, and for composing the index. The author is usually responsible for permissions, figures, and indexes, although textbook publishers generally prefer to handle these tasks.

- Contracts usually describe how future editions of the book will be handled. Many contracts give publishers the right to request a revised edition of the book. If you don't want to revise the book, the contract gives publishers the ability to commission another author to revise it. This clause isn't as bad as it sounds. If you pass away or retire the publisher can continue to sell and promote the book. The contract might outline adjustments in royalties—either increases or decreases—for future editions.

- The contract will specify who owns the copyright to the book. For scholarly books, the publisher typically retains the copyright. The publisher will also describe what happens to the book if it goes out of print. A contract might stipulate, for example, that the author can request a reprinting if the book has been out of print for 6 months. If the publisher declines to reprint the book, then the publisher must reassign all rights to the author. Be sure that you own the rights to the book when it goes out of print. That gives you the option of revising the book and reprinting it with a different publisher.

- A publisher may put a *right of first refusal* clause in the contract. This clause means that they want to have the first shot at your next book proposal, even if they decide not to publish your next book.

DEALING WITH THE DETAILS

When your book reaches its natural end, you'll need to drag yourself away from the joy of writing so you can attend to the greater joys of preparing to deliver the book to the publisher. Your editor will send you guidelines that describe how you should prepare the book. In this stage, you'll gather your permissions forms, make high-quality electronic figures, and fill any small gaps in the text and references that were too boring to do in the first place. The publisher will send you an extensive author questionnaire that asks for information about you and about your book. This information is used for cataloging, marketing, and promotion, so you should put a lot of thought into it. You may be asked to suggest cover art and scholars who might provide blurbs. And fire up your laser printer, because publishers typically want several hard copies along with an electronic copy.

When your book enters production, expect big packages of copyedited manuscript and page proofs from the production editor—your figurative bundle of joy will resemble a real bundle. Most books are on a tight production schedule; don't drop the ball now. Remember that advance you got? Spend a few hundred dollars of it to pay someone to review your page proofs. You'll read the proofs, of course, but you should get a second reader with fresh eyes. A good friend who worked as a copyeditor read the proofs for my first book; a graduate student who worked at my university's writing center read the proofs for my second book. If you need to prepare the indexes, you'll make those when you receive the proofs. The tedium of indexing will test your resolve, but it will build authorial character.

Conclusions

Writing books is clean family fun without the fun or family (or even the cleanliness if you spill your coffee like I do). There is no ineluctable mystery to book writing, just the eluctable routine of following your writing schedule. People read books when they want to learn about a new area, to gain a broad perspective on a body of research, and to see what you have to say. If you have something to say, write a book. If you have a lot to say, write two. When you start writing a book, send me an e-mail and let me know how it's going. I'd like to hear how these tips worked for you and if you have any suggestions for aspiring book writers.

8

"The Good Things Still to Be Written"

This book has proposed a practical system for becoming a productive academic writer. Chapter 2 bulldozed some specious barriers to writing a lot and introduced the system's core feature: writing according to a schedule. To help you follow your schedule, chapters 3 and 4 described how to set good goals and priorities, how to monitor your writing, and how to start an agraphia group. Chapter 5 set you on the path to writing well, and chapters 6 and 7 offered practical tips for writing journal articles and books. It's ironic to write a short book about how to write a lot, but there isn't much to say. The system is simple.

THE JOY OF SCHEDULING

The joys of following a writing schedule are many and obvious. You'll write more pages per week, which translates into more journal articles, more grant proposals, more book chapters, and more books. Following a schedule eliminates the uncertainties and sorrows of

"It's plotted out. I just have to write it."

"finding time to write," of wondering if something will get done. Projects will wrap up well before their deadlines. You'll spend as much time writing during the summer weeks as you'll spend during the first weeks of class: A writing schedule flattens your writing output into a pleasing rectangular distribution. Writing will become mundane, routine, and typical, not oppressive, uncertain, and monopolistic.

An unexpected joy of following a schedule is a craftsman's sense of pride. The external rewards for writing are few and unpredictable—occasionally an acceptance letter pokes through the pile of rejections. The internal rewards are even fewer for binge writers. Motivated by guilt and anxiety, binge writers don't find the process of writing rewarding. Because of the long binge, the writing period is followed by a burnt-out haze that confirms the binge writer's distaste of writing. When you stick to a schedule, a behaviorist might say, you take control of your schedule of reinforcement (Skinner, 1987). You know when you will be rewarded for meeting your goal. My goal is to write every weekday morning. Some days I get a lot done; other days are grim and frustrating. But even on the bad days, I'm happy that I sat down and did it: I proudly type a "1" into my SPSS file, and I give myself a figurative pat on the back (embodied as a cup of good coffee). I didn't want to write—the urge to go out for bagels is sometimes strong—but I did anyway. After following my schedule for so long, this small daily victory, not the prospect of distal publication, motivates my writing.

Less Wanting, More Doing

You don't need special traits, special genes, or special motivation to write a lot. You don't need to want to write—people rarely feel like doing unpleasant tasks that lack deadlines—so don't wait until you feel like it. Productive writing involves harnessing the power of habit, and habits come from repetition. Make a schedule and sit down to write during your scheduled time. You might spend the first few sessions cursing, groaning, and gnashing your teeth, but at least you're cursing during your scheduled time and not in binges.

After a couple of weeks, your writing schedule will become habitual, and you'll no longer feel pressured to write during nonscheduled hours. And once your writing schedule ossifies into a sturdy routine, the notion of "wanting to write" will strike you as perplexing and mysterious. The force of habit will make you sit down and start to write.

Ironically, writing a lot will not make you enjoy writing or want to write. Writing is hard and it will always be hard; writing is unpleasant and it will always be unpleasant. Most days, I don't want to sit in my hard fiberglass chair, turn on my computer, and confront a half-completed manuscript. But teaching can be frustrating, too, and slogging through tedious committee meetings is maddening. How do people deal with those tasks? They just show up. Make a writing schedule and show up for it. Want less and do more. "Decide what you want to do," wrote William Zinsser. "Then decide to do it. Then do it" (Zinsser, 2001, p. 285).

WRITING ISN'T A RACE

Write as much or as little as you want to write. Although this book shows you how to write a lot, don't think that you ought to write a lot. A more accurate title for this book would be *How to Write More Productively During the Normal Work Week With Less Anxiety and Guilt*, but no one would buy that book. If you want to write more, a writing schedule will make you a more productive writer. You'll spend more hours per week writing, and you'll write more efficiently. Eventually, you'll plow through your backlog of unpublished data and write with more confidence. If you don't want to write more, a writing schedule will take the guilt and uncertainty out of writing. You won't worry about "finding time to write," and you won't sacrifice your weekends for wasteful writing binges. If you plan to write only a few things in your life, your writing time can be thinking time. Use your scheduled writing time to read good books and to think about your professional development.

Publishing a lot does not make you a good person, psychologist, or scientist. Some of psychology's most prolific writers rehash the same ideas ceaselessly: Empirical articles lead to a couple of review articles, the review articles are rewarmed as book chapters, and the book chapters are retreaded as handbook chapters and newsletter articles. Prolific writers have more publications, but they don't necessarily have more good ideas than anyone else. Writing isn't a race. Don't publish a paper just for the sake of having one more published paper. Don't count your publications. Be proud of the euthanized manuscripts—papers that could be published somewhere but shouldn't be published anywhere—lurking in your file cabinet. If you find yourself counting notches on your academic bedpost, spend a writing period thinking about your motives and goals.

Enjoy Life

A writing schedule brings balance to your life—not *balance* in the pseudoscientific, New Age, self-help sense of wondrous fulfillment, but *balance* in the sense of separating work and play. Binge writers foolishly search for big chunks of time, and they "find" this time during the evenings and weekends. Binge writing thus consumes time that should be spent on normal living. Is academic writing more important than spending time with your family and friends, petting the dog, and drinking coffee? A dog unpetted is a sad dog; a cup of coffee forsaken is caffeine lost forever. Protect your real-world time just as you protect your scheduled writing time. Spend your evenings and weekends hanging out with your family and friends, building canoes, bidding on vintage Alvar Aalto furniture that you don't need, watching *Law & Order* reruns, repainting the shutters, or teaching your cat to use the toilet. It doesn't matter what you do as long as you don't spend your free time writing—there's time during the work week for that.

The End

This book is over; thanks for reading it. I enjoyed writing this book, but it's time for me to write something else, and it's time for you to write something, too. Let's look forward to it. "When I think of the good things still to be written I am glad," wrote William Saroyan, "for there is no end to them, and I know I myself shall write some of them" (Saroyan, 1952, p. 2).

Good Books About Writing

The Few Essential Books

American Psychological Association. (2001). *Publication manual of the American Psychological Association* (5th ed.). Washington, DC: Author.

Merriam-Webster's collegiate dictionary (11th ed.). Springfield, MA: Merriam-Webster.[1]

Strunk, W., Jr., & White, E. B. (2000). *The elements of style* (4th ed.). New York: Longman.

Zinsser, W. (2001). *On writing well* (25th anniversary ed.). New York: Quill.

Books for Style

Baker, S. (1969). *The practical stylist* (2nd ed.). New York: Thomas Y. Crowell.

---

[1] This or any other good dictionary.

Barzun, J. (2001). *Simple and direct: A rhetoric for writers*. New York: HarperCollins.

Harris, R. W. (2003). *When good people write bad sentences: 12 steps to better writing habits*. New York: St. Martin's Press.

Smith, K. (2001). *Junk English*. New York: Blast Books.

Smith, K. (2004). *Junk English 2*. New York: Blast Books.

Walsh, B. (2000). *Lapsing into a comma: A curmudgeon's guide to the many things that can go wrong in print—And how to avoid them*. New York: Contemporary Books.

Walsh, B. (2004). *The elephants of style: A trunkload of tips on the big issues and gray areas of contemporary American English*. New York: McGraw-Hill.

Books for Grammar and Punctuation

Gordon, K. E. (1984). *The transitive vampire: A handbook of grammar for the innocent, the eager, and the doomed*. New York: Times Books.

Gordon, K. E. (2003). *The new well-tempered sentence: A punctuation handbook for the innocent, the eager, and the doomed*. Boston: Mariner.

Hale, C. (1999). *Sin and syntax: How to craft wickedly effective prose*. New York: Broadway.

Truss, L. (2003). *Eats, shoots & leaves: The zero tolerance approach to punctuation*. New York: Gotham.

BOOKS FOR MOTIVATION

Boice, R. (1990). *Professors as writers: A self-help guide to productive writing.* Stillwater, OK: New Forums Press.

Friedman, B. (1993). *Writing past dark: Envy, fear, distraction, and other dilemmas in the writer's life.* New York: HarperCollins.

Keyes, R. (2003). *The writer's book of hope.* New York: Holt.

King, S. (2000). *On writing: A memoir of the craft.* New York: Scribner.

References

Allport, G. W. (1961). *Pattern and growth in personality*. New York: Holt, Rinehart & Winston.

American Psychological Association. (2001). *Publication manual of the American Psychological Association* (5th ed.). Washington, DC: Author.

Atkinson, J. W. (1964). *An introduction to motivation*. New York: Van Nostrand.

Baker, S. (1969). *The practical stylist* (2nd ed.). New York: Thomas Y. Crowell.

Bandura, A. (1997). *Self-efficacy: The exercise of control*. New York: Freeman.

Batson, C. D., Schoenrade, P., & Ventis, W. L. (1993). *Religion and the individual*. New York: Oxford University Press.

Baumeister, R. F., & Leary, M. R. (1997). Writing narrative literature reviews. *Review of General Psychology, 1*, 311–320.

Bem, D. J. (1995). Writing a review article for *Psychological Bulletin*. *Psychological Bulletin, 118*, 172–177.

Boice, R. (1990). *Professors as writers: A self-help guide to productive writing*. Stillwater, OK: New Forums Press.

Brehm, J. W. (1966). *A theory of psychological reactance*. New York: Academic Press.

Carver, C. S., & Scheier, M. F. (1998). *On the self-regulation of behavior*. New York: Cambridge University Press.

Cooper, H. (2003). Editorial. *Psychological Bulletin, 129*, 3–9.

Duval, T. S., & Silvia, P. J. (2001). *Self-awareness and causal attribution: A dual systems theory*. Boston: Kluwer Academic.

Duval, T. S., & Wicklund, R. A. (1972). *A theory of objective self-awareness*. New York: Academic Press.

Eisenberg, N. (2000). Writing a literature review. In R. J. Sternberg (Ed.), *Guide to publishing in psychology journals* (pp. 17–34). Cambridge, England: Cambridge University Press.

Ericsson, K. A., Krampe, R. T., & Tesch-Römer, C. (1993). The role of deliberate practice in the acquisition of expert performance. *Psychological Review, 100*, 363–406.

Gordon, K. E. (2003). *The new well-tempered sentence: A punctuation handbook for the innocent, the eager, and the doomed*. Boston: Mariner.

Grawe, S. (2005). Live/work. *Dwell, 5*(5), 76–80.

Hale, C. (1999). *Sin and syntax: How to craft wickedly effective prose*. New York: Broadway.

Heider, F. (1958). *The psychology of interpersonal relations*. New York: Wiley.

Hull, C. L. (1943). *Principles of behavior*. New York: Appleton-Century-Crofts.

Jellison, J. M. (1993). *Overcoming resistance: A practical guide to producing change in the workplace*. New York: Simon & Schuster.

Kellogg, R. T. (1994). *The psychology of writing*. New York: Oxford University Press.

Kendall, P. C., Silk, J. S., & Chu, B. C. (2000). Introducing your research report: Writing the introduction. In R. J. Sternberg (Ed.), *Guide to publishing in psychology journals* (pp. 41–57). Cambridge, England: Cambridge University Press.

Keyes, R. (2003). *The writer's book of hope*. New York: Holt.

King, S. (2000). *On writing: A memoir of the craft*. New York: Scribner.

Kline, R. B. (2005). *Principles and practice of structural equation modeling* (2nd ed.). New York: Guilford Press.

Korotitsch, W. J., & Nelson-Gray, R. O. (1999). An overview of self-monitoring research in assessment and treatment. *Psychological Assessment, 11*, 415–425.

Lewin, K. (1935). *A dynamic theory of personality*. New York: McGraw-Hill.

Parrott, A. C. (1999). Does cigarette smoking cause stress? *American Psychologist, 54*, 817–820.

Pope-Hennessy, J. (1971). *Anthony Trollope*. London: Phoenix Press.

Reis, H. T. (2000). Writing effectively about design. In R. J. Sternberg (Ed.), *Guide to publishing in psychology journals* (pp. 81–97). Cambridge, England: Cambridge University Press.

Salovey, P. (2000). Results that get results: Telling a good story. In R. J. Sternberg (Ed.), *Guide to publishing in psychology journals* (pp. 121–132). Cambridge, England: Cambridge University Press.

Saroyan, W. (1952). *A bicycle rider in Beverly Hills*. New York: Scribner.

Sawyer, R. K. (2006). *Explaining creativity: The science of human innovation*. New York: Oxford University Press.

Silvia, P. J. (2006). *Exploring the psychology of interest*. New York: Oxford University Press.

Silvia, P. J., & Gendolla, G. H. E. (2001). On introspection and self-perception: Does self-focused attention enable accurate self-knowledge? *Review of General Psychology, 5,* 241–269.

Skinner, B. F. (1987). *Upon further reflection*. Englewood Cliffs, NJ: Prentice Hall.

Smith, K. (2001). *Junk English*. New York: Blast Books.

Sternberg, R. J. (Ed.). (2000). *Guide to publishing in psychology journals*. Cambridge, England: Cambridge University Press.

Strunk, W., Jr., & White, E. B. (2000). *The elements of style* (4th ed.). New York: Longman.

Stumpf, B. (2000). *The ice palace that melted away: How good design enhances our lives*. Minneapolis: University of Minnesota Press.

Trollope, A. (1999). *An autobiography*. New York: Oxford University Press. (Original work published 1883)

Wrightsman, L. S. (1999). *Judicial decision making: Is psychology relevant?* Boston: Kluwer Academic.

Wrightsman, L. S., & Fulero, S. M. (2004). *Forensic psychology* (2nd ed.). Belmont, CA: Wadsworth.

Zinsser, W. (1988). *Writing to learn*. New York: Quill.

Zinsser, W. (2001). *On writing well* (25th anniversary ed.). New York: Quill.

Index

About the Author

Paul J. Silvia received his PhD in psychology from the University of Kansas in 2001. He studies the psychology of emotion, particularly what makes things interesting, the role of emotions in the arts, and how emotions intersect with personality. He received the Berlyne Award, an early-career award given by American Psychological Association Division 10 (Society for the Psychology of Aesthetics, Creativity, and the Arts), for his research on aesthetic emotions. Dr. Silvia is the author of *Exploring the Psychology of Interest* (2006) and *Self-Awareness and Causal Attribution* (with T. S. Duval, 2001). In his free time, he drinks coffee; pets Lia, his Bernese mountain dog; and enjoys not writing.